D0193161

WHAT WE KNOW

WHAT WE KNOW

SOLUTIONS FROM OUR EXPERIENCES
IN THE JUSTICE SYSTEM

EDITED BY

VIVIAN NIXON AND DARYL V. ATKINSON

THE
NEW
PRESS

NEW YORK
LONDON

Requests for permission to reproduce selections from this book should be made
through our website: https://thenewpress.com/contact.

Published in the United States by The New Press, New York, 2020
Distributed by Two Rivers Distribution

ISBN 978-1-62097-529-9 (hc)
ISBN 978-1-62097-530-5 (ebook)
CIP data is available

The New Press publishes books that promote and enrich public discussion and
understanding of the issues vital to our democracy and to a more equitable world.
These books are made possible by the enthusiasm of our readers; the support
of a committed group of donors, large and small; the collaboration of our many
partners in the independent media and the not-for-profit sector; booksellers, who
often hand-sell New Press books; librarians; and above all by our authors.

www.thenewpress.com

Published in consultation with the Center for American Progress and the Formerly
Incarcerated Convicted Peoples and Families Movement.

The views expressed herein are those of the authors and do not necessarily
represent those of CAP or FICPFM.

Book design and composition by Bookbright Media
This book was set in Palatino and Alternate Gothic 2

Printed in the United States of America

10 9 8 7 6 5 4 3 2 1

Contents

Introduction

Vivian Nixon and Daryl V. Atkinson

Far too many people can rattle off the numbers describing the problems of the criminal legal system with startling ease:* almost 2.3 million people are confined in prisons and jails across the United States today; one in three black men born today will be imprisoned in their lives; over the last forty years the number of incarcerated women has increased by more than 700 percent; more than seventy million Americans are living with a criminal record.[1] It is easy to take these numbers at face value and read past them without acknowledging the human meaning behind them. The statistics come across as sterile and impersonal. But for us, this problem is deeply personal.

We each spent more than three years in prison. We each had our experience coming face-to-face with the reality that

---

people in poverty, people of color, and those without access to education and opportunity are grossly overrepresented in the criminal legal system. And, unlike many of the men and women we were incarcerated with, we both had support systems to welcome us home. Whether it was a family to provide us with the most immediate needs of food, shelter, and clothing, or an organizational support system like College and Community Fellowship, we both had the opportunity to pursue a higher education upon release. We earned our degrees— one in law, the other in nonprofit management followed by an MFA—and have since dedicated our careers to advocating for justice reform. We served our sentences and we came home with a deep understanding, not just of the failures of the criminal legal system, but also the infinite potential of the people who are relegated to our country's prisons and jails.

Most Americans agree that the criminal legal system must be transformed if it is to become a system of justice. But only a select group of people have been invited to the table to imagine innovative solutions. People with conviction histories are barred from access to education and employment, and in many states are denied the right to vote. Basic tools that are necessary to advocate for oneself are out of reach for most people who have been involved in the criminal legal system. The designation "criminal justice reform expert" has been narrowly attributed to academics and practitioners—the lawyers, judges, police, and politicians. But those perspectives often see only one side of this complex problem. To our detriment, we as a country have largely failed to recognize the expertise and potential of incarcerated people and people with conviction histories.

That is why, since coming home, we've dedicated our

careers not just to fixing the system but to amplifying the voices of those who are closest to the problem. Now, one of us leads the very same organization that was there in a time of need, College and Community Fellowship, which helps women who have been affected by the criminal legal system to earn their college degrees so that they, their families, and their communities can thrive. The other runs Forward Justice, which advances racial, social, and economic justice by partnering with human rights organizations at the forefront of social movements in the U.S. South. Together, we serve on the steering committee of the Formerly Incarcerated, Convicted People's and Family Movement—a network of over fifty civil and human rights organizations that are led by people living with criminal records and their family members.

We believe that directly impacted people can bring the solutions to that transformation we seek. The voices of currently and formerly incarcerated people are so much more than the traumas we've experienced. Those who have not been directly impacted should respect our expertise, listen to what we have to say, and take the opportunity to step back and allow us to lead a movement for change.

Justice-involved people have been the source of many policy ideas that are now considered central tenets of criminal justice reform, but our contributions have often gone unrecognized. Ban the Box, for example, the campaign to remove the check box that asks a job candidate about their conviction history, was developed by a coalition of formerly incarcerated people who had experienced discrimination in hiring and struggled to get jobs; since the movement began in 2003, over 150 cities and the majority of states have implemented Ban the Box policies.[2] In 2018, Desmond Meade, a person with a criminal history, led a collaborative campaign that restored voting rights to 1.4 million Floridians. The erasure of citizenship, and the sense of invisibility it triggered, drove thousands of activists to demand the right to civic participation.[3]

The essays in this book offer ideas to change policy and practice in the criminal legal system. All the authors are currently or formerly incarcerated. Some suggest bold sweeping transformations, and others aim to change a specific practice that is centered in the author's experience. They are compiled from an open call for submissions to writers inside and outside of prisons and jails. The only requirements were that authors be currently or formerly incarcerated and that they propose a policy solution connected to their direct experience with the justice system. In just four months we received over three hundred essays from thirty-five states across the country. We handpicked the twenty-three pieces collected here—concrete solutions to some of the hardest and ugliest problems in the criminal legal system.

In this book you hear from a man, currently incarcerated in Indiana, who proposes a Prison Labor Standards Act, calling for an end to prison slave labor and a greater respect for the dignity of incarcerated workers. You also hear from a Nebraska man who served a federal prison term for white-collar crimes, and now has a proposal for offering courses in entrepreneurship as a way to break down barriers to employment for people returning from incarceration. A formerly incarcerated woman who now leads a nationally prominent justice reform organization pleads for greater empathy in understanding the human dignity of justice-involved individuals. And a man serving a twenty-five-year term for a crime he committed at age fifteen powerfully advocates for getting rid of existing financial incentives to charge youths as adults. These and the other essays in this volume lay bare the truth of how deeply flawed our current system is. And each essay uses the author's personal story to draw a line to a policy solution that would bring a degree of dignity, fairness, and actual justice to this nation's criminal legal system. We acknowledge that some of the authors included here have caused harm to others, but the underlying foundation of this work is that those actions do not negate their expertise and ability to develop sound and profoundly necessary policy recommendations.

We, the editors of this book, do not necessarily agree with every aspect of every reform suggested in these pages—often, we do not feel they go far enough. For instance, Aaron Striz in chapter 5 advocates for a "20/20" plan, making parole a possibility for people who were incarcerated in their teens and have completed twenty or more years in prison—we think that a twenty-year sentence for a teen is excessive and out of step with the rest of the world; we would not want to see that become an acceptable minimum before parole is considered. Likewise, in chapter 16, Sreedhar Potarazu advocates for more basic literacy instruction in prison, which we endorse, but also suggests adding illiteracy as a factor to be considered in risk assessments, which we do not endorse. We were struck by the very modest nature of some of the proposed reforms, which seem to speak to a disturbing acceptance of a disproportionately punitive system. And we were surprised and disheartened not to receive any submissions calling for the complete abolition of prisons and detention centers, though this may have been a function of the way we worded our initial request for proposals—including the idea that we hoped for new reform ideas not currently in circulation. All of that said, our approach was not to solicit pieces with particular arguments, but to defer to the contributors in proposing their reforms and to practice what the book preaches about listening to and respecting the wisdom of "those who know."

We hope that these ideas ground you in the understanding that no one should be defined by their mistakes alone. Civil rights lawyer Bryan Stevenson said, "Proximity has taught me some basic and humbling truths, including this vital lesson: *Each of us is more than the worst thing we've ever done.*"[4] This book—in fact all of our work—is rooted in the principle that every person has great potential if only it is nurtured and given the opportunity to flourish. We hope that currently and formerly incarcerated people and people with conviction histories will read this book and see it as proof that we have a central role in the fight for reform. We hope that policy makers will take this book as a call to action to implement policies in their own institutions and intentionally bring directly impacted people to their decision-making tables.

Collectively, we have reached a critical point where the justice reform movement can no longer ignore or discount the voices of the people who are most intimately familiar with the criminal legal system. We must be front and center in the fight to end mass incarceration because we bring the necessary urgency and innovative strength that the movement requires. This is what we know, and we know it better than anyone else.

A Note from the Editors

We would like to take a moment to note the importance of language. Language commonly used to describe people who have been involved with the criminal legal system can often be dehumanizing and degrading. We as editors hold ourselves and our colleagues to a standard of using people-first language, including people who are: currently/formerly incarcerated, justice-involved, directly impacted, or system impacted. American society-at-large has become overly accustomed to using terms that strip dignity and identity from people with conviction histories by using words like inmate, convict, or felon. However, we defer to each individual author in this book on their preferred language to describe themself and those with whom they are or have been incarcerated. As such, this book employs a wide variety of terms.

Additionally, it is important for the reader to understand that this book draws the connection between personal experience and policy development. Each essay reflects the author's own research and personal recollections. Each essay describes events in the author's lives as truthfully as recollection permits and/or can be verified by research. We commend each of these authors for their willingness to share their stories and join with us in this endeavor to center the voices of people who have been directly impacted by the justice system.

—*Vivian Nixon and Daryl V. Atkinson*

1

Earmark Jobs to Reduce Recidivism

Kevin E. Jackmon

Kevin Jackmon is currently serving a life sentence in Massachusetts for armed robbery and felony murder. Jackmon experienced first-hand the consequences of a criminal conviction after his first stint of incarceration, when he was paroled in 1995 and unable to find a job despite his experience and skills as a machinist in the U.S. Navy. To combat recidivism, he proposes to earmark entry-level state jobs for returning citizens in automotive repair, culinary arts, cosmetology, barbering, landscaping, farming, and construction.

Have you ever been convicted of a felony?

In 1995, after being paroled on a drug distribution conviction, I applied for a position at a pool, plumbing, and pipe-fitting company for which I was uniquely qualified. Four years as a machinist mate in the U.S. Navy had immersed me in engineering. A school and C school training, hundreds of repair orders known as "2-Kilos," and countless hours of preventative maintenance had given me knowledge of engineering tolerances less than one-thousandth of an inch, boiler main feed pumps capable of 1,200-foot-pound steam at 975 degrees, and other highly specialized professional expertise. I also possessed intimate knowledge of almost every type of valve known to man. The owner of the small pipe-fitting company concluded my interview by saying: "Kevin, you're the most impressive applicant I've interviewed all day. I have one more interview and two open positions. You pass the background check and I'll guarantee you fifteen dollars an hour starting next Monday."

Needless to say, I never heard from him again.

In the weeks that ensued, I trudged through additional interviews at different companies, only to get the same result. Potential employers were sufficiently impressed by my qualifications, but were similarly disappointed to learn of my thirty-two-month incarceration.

Have you ever been convicted of a felony?

My transformation from ex-military to ex-con, pipe fitter to re-offender, follows a pattern many others like me have experienced because of the difficulties of bouncing back from that first misstep, that first criminal conviction. Thousands of citizens have committed petty or nonviolent crimes, done their time, and then struggled to find gainful employment, only to fall back on their tendencies toward crime after encountering obstacles they could not overcome. A prior conviction is the job seeker's albatross, a scarlet letter on every application, thwarting a desire to do right.[1]

Have you ever been convicted of a felony?

With a little foresight, frugality, and a big change in thinking, the justice system and society in general can dismantle this particular obstacle, effectively reducing the soaring rate of recidivism. My personal experience and insight as a recidivist has helped me identify certain policies that can be implemented to help released inmates become productive members of society and avoid re-offending.

For one, education and vocational training should be mandatory for inmates within two years of their release date. Focusing resources on instruction in occupations where background takes a backseat to skill prepares inmates to acquire good-paying jobs, increasing their chances of overall success and in turn reducing their likelihood of re-offending. Fields well suited for this include automotive repair, culinary arts, cosmetology, barbering, landscaping, farming, and construction trades.

Additionally, a state's legislature should earmark a percentage of state jobs for *ex-cons only*. Designated entry-level jobs should be obtainable through some type of post-release supervision, perhaps probation or parole, and be spread throughout the state so as not to be concentrated in any one community or town. (The number of jobs for this group would be equivalent to only 1 percent of the state's inmate population.) The number of available positions should increase or decrease in proportion to current inmate population levels. The positions should offer the same pay, benefits, and opportunities for advancement as do positions occupied by employees without criminal records. This will allow ex-offenders to prove themselves and gain the experience necessary to move on to other employment opportunities. States can reduce the 1 percent commitment by contracting an appropriate number of private companies to hire ex-cons in return for tax breaks and other incentives, such as reduced utility rates or improved infrastructure.

And finally, certain private-sector job applications should be purged of any questions inquiring about or in any way identifying prior convictions. No more *Have you ever been convicted of a felony?* on applications for entry-level positions. A commonsense approach is necessary to achieve the main goal of providing ex-cons with employment opportunities without enticing anyone to re-offend. Victim-sensitive jobs, such as positions at day cares, schools, banks, and so on, will require exemptions. No one is proposing a child molester take on crossing guard duty, or a bank robber drive for Brink's.

Detractors may protest the merits of employing an ex-con over someone without a criminal background, to which I say: the vast majority of incarcerated persons will leave prison someday. It's better to employ them rather than avoid them. Would an average citizen rather encounter an ex-con who's gainfully employed and legally earning an income or one who's unemployed and forced to obtain funds illegally? Consider the robbery I eventually committed after numerous failed attempts to get a job upon my release. My crime had a direct impact on over twenty people—employees, patrons, and first responders—putting them in a life-or-death situation; everyone, including me, was affected, including family and friends. That's hundreds of people adversely affected because potential employers refused to overlook my sale of two dime bags of marijuana.

I am not shifting blame here: my choice, my actions led to consequences—period. However, had I been gainfully employed, I would not have resorted to robbing a restaurant. Money was my motive, and fifteen dollars an hour would have been enough to make my crime unnecessary. Working—plumbing pools and repairing boilers—would have kept me from taking the incremental steps that eventually led me to commit an ill-advised robbery and reenter prison.

Imagine implementing the above suggestions: training inmates in conviction-friendly occupations, allocating state jobs for ex-offenders, and deleting conviction indicators on job applications. Doing this for one hundred inmates could prevent hundreds of crimes—that's thousands of everyday citizens *not* adversely affected, thousands of people *not* becoming victims, thousands living a happier life in a more peaceful world because hundreds of inmates returned to the workforce instead of to crime.

2

A Tiny Ray of Light: On the Need for an Authentic Oversight Regime Within the Texas Department of Criminal Justice

Thomas Bartlett Whitaker

Thomas Bartlett Whitaker is the founder and editor of Minutes Before Six, *a nonprofit literary journal for prison writers. He is a three-time first-place winner in the essay and fiction categories of the PEN Prison Writing Contest and was named a PEN Writing for Justice Fellow in October 2018. His essay "A Nothing Would Do As Well" was included in the New Press anthology* Hell Is a Very Small Place. *During his time behind bars he graduated summa cum laude with a BA in sociology and English from Adams State University and received his MA in humanities from California State University. Whitaker is currently serving a life sentence in Texas and proposes to create Independent Monitoring Boards in every detention center for sentencing accountability.*

Pretend you are in a cell. Seriously, just for one moment. Steel door, steel toilet; concrete walls furry from a dozen paint jobs, with every paint flake racing to unpeel itself first; a tiny window, if you are lucky. Graffiti and burn marks cover everything, and there's an awful smell that you slowly begin to realize is coming from feces squirted into the vent, a gift left behind from a previous occupant. For a second, try to project yourself into that place. It is important to exercise your imagination. You have to be able to feel the sheer trepanning god-awfulness of this world before you can really begin to think about it.

Perhaps this seems suspiciously sentimental, embarrassingly unacademic; you may be accustomed to there being a comfortable distance set between where you stand and what you study. We need to surgically remove that false sense of security you feel when you think about America's prison system. As Susan Sontag well knew, "wherever people feel safe . . . they will be indifferent."[1] And, frankly, your indifference is killing us. I've read your monographs, your peer-reviewed journals, your white papers. My inner Spock appreciates your erudition, but you still aren't getting it—not really. It's still not entirely real to you yet. You see the fish, and you see the harpoon plunging toward them through the water, but you are not taking the refraction angle into account.

How do I know you aren't hitting your target? I know because things are getting worse instead of better. Day in, day out, the level of disorderliness in the system spirals downward, and all of you are still chuckling over prison rape jokes. "Prison reform" is jargon in your world. It is a fantasy in mine, a cruel, loathsome dream that punches me in the heart every single time I start to believe that someone out there might have a chance of changing anything.

Focus on the cell. Say they dumped you in an ad-seg wing ("administrative segregation," a term for solitary confinement). Let's ignore the big questions about exactly why you find yourself in such a place. Let's stick to the minor issues you are going to be faced with, the daily annoyances that constitute and define a life in a Texas prison. I know you are going to be tempted to keep elevating your sight to the Texas Department of Criminal Justice's whole essence or *Dasein* or whatever, but that is folly—trust me. Nietzsche got more than a little wrong over the course of his oeuvre, but he was spot on when it came to the business of staring into abysses. All you have to do to know the truth is talk to a correctional officer with a few years of experience in these carceral depths; trust me, you will understand what time in ad-seg means in all its horrid truth within a few weeks of your arrival. Watch your feet for now, take small steps—but be careful, because everything here is slippery.

That guy screaming downstairs? Don't try to parse the actual content of his tirade, because he's insane. He needs help. In a blue state, he'd be in some kind of hospital, but down here in the Yee-Haw Republic, we don't want to pay taxes for that sort of thing, so seg is the rug under which we sweep such souls. Ignore him, and buy some earplugs. Keep going: yes, yes, it's winter now and you still haven't received a jacket or a blanket. You can send all the I-60s in the world, but you're better off trying to buy what you need on the black market—the "street," in patois.* If you give up your rec and shower for a few days, the officers will break the rules and pass a jacket or blanket to you from one of the other convicts, once you've come to an arrangement with someone. In the meantime, do some push-ups or something to stay warm. What else? No, don't even mention the chow. Nutritious and tasty food is for civilians, and you are a convict now. It wasn't that long ago that people like us were considered *civiliter mortuus*† here in the South, dead to the law, literal slaves to the state, devoid even of the right to have rights. You aren't getting your medication? Your cell is infested with roaches, literally dozens of them no matter which direction you face? You prepared an essay for publication, and when you tried to mail it out the first time, they "disappeared" it, immediately shipped you to a different unit, and then "lost" the portion of your property that contained your early drafts and supporting documentation? An officer wrote you a nonsense disciplinary citation because his boss instituted a quota? Welcome to the penitentiary. Now, how do you think you'll prove that any of these things actually happened to you, when the prison system itself is going to claim that you are a liar?

I know what you are thinking: there has to be some sort of accountability structure in this wasteland of hostile indifference, right? Ah yes, there's the rub. The purpose of this whole foray into fiction was to grind a single point into your face: there isn't a single policy change in the whole wide universe

---

* An I-60 is a Texas Department of Corrections form for any kind of request to an official, for example, a medical visit, a change in diet, or a contact visit.

† Latin for "civil death."

of reform discourse that you can propose, debate, lobby for, legislate, or codify into statute that matters in the tiniest way, unless the chasm between what exists on paper and what actually takes place inside the walls is bridged. Right now, that gap is astronomical. It is so wide that by the time light from your world reaches ours, it feels like it came from a star that died eons ago.

The only way to connect these two realities is for the prisons in Texas to be forced to operate under the gaze of an independent monitor. Right now, the only people watching are the prisons themselves. (I keep reading cheap clichés being tossed around in the newspapers about "foxes guarding henhouses," which feels imbecilic to me. The truth is we'd all love to deal with human foxes. Even rabid human wolves with lasers attached to their mutant snouts would be a vast improvement to what currently exists.) What this means in practice is that policy equates to whatever the big man with the steel baton says it does, period. If you don't like what King Redneck the First has to say about the matter, well, he's got a five-man Extraction Team* ready to show you the errors in your valuational perspective.

Positing the need for additional oversight is a bit like wishing for a universal cure for cancer: an easy, obvious thing to desire, but a vastly improbable target to actually hit. I offer no panaceas here, because living in this place has cured me of a belief in such things. A truly independent monitoring regime, imbued with genuine power to correct flaws in the

---

* A team of corrections officers who specialize in using force to remove individuals from their cells and searching for and confiscating contraband.

administration of our prisons, must be viewed as a goal for the future, for a time when the motivation-method-opportunity triad seems more apt. At best, what I think we need to focus on is a multi-phased approach in which our first objective is a relatively modest one: figuring out a way to insert as many non-department-aligned eyeballs into this side of the fence as possible, even if these witnesses spend a limited number of hours inside the facility and have little authority to change policy. As I will explain below, I suspect this could produce a number of profound effects on the status quo. Before we can go hunting for such a rare beast, however, we need to burn the underbrush a little to get a better view of the terrain. In particular, we need to remove the stumps of the current tripartite monitoring regime, because these mechanisms are not merely useless, but upon close inspection appear to have been designed to be so: a set of genuine placebos, to mix metaphors.

The first layer of unit oversight is the Administrative Grievance Program, located within the Texas bureaucracy in the Risk Management Division.[2] Wait, what "risk" are we talking about, you might innocently wonder. Why, the risk of the system getting smacked upside the head by a civil rights lawsuit, of course. The ruse works in the following manner: Say a corrections officer doesn't like you and decides to stop feeding you during his shifts. You have fifteen days to file a grievance on him. If you go over this mark by even one second, the issue becomes moot. Because the Prison Litigation Reform Act requires inmates to exhaust the administrative resolution process before a Title 42, Section 1983 suit can be filed in federal district court, this essentially means that the prison system has a mere fifteen-day liability horizon for anything it does to inmates.³ Anything beyond this is time-barred, or runs the risk of having the courts grant summary judgment for the state due to a failure to appropriately attempt administrative resolution. Nowhere else in the U.S. but our prisons can one find such a minimal time window of accountability.

While this may seem awfully suspect to some of you, the Fifth Circuit hasn't been particularly troubled by the matter, to put things lightly. The program claims in its mission statement, "Our decisions are not always popular, but we pride ourselves in 'doing the right thing.'" You can probably guess which part of that statement most inmates might agree with.

Only three types of prisoners even bother with the program: fresh convicts just hopping off Charon's dinghy who still erroneously believe in institutions; utter masochists, the quixotic depravity of whom has reached proportions beyond description—at least in the view of this humble wordsmith; and prisoners intending to file a lawsuit down the road. Huge numbers of my peers have never even filed a single grievance, and never will. A 2008 audit report by the state auditor's office on the grievance program makes it very clear why this state of unwillingness obtains: 62 percent of a total of 1,641 prisoners surveyed at seven prisons reported having previously faced retaliation for filing a grievance, and 35 percent said they were afraid to file because of fear of retaliation.⁴ Given that the process usually involves nothing more than the grievance officer sharing the grievance form with the corrections officer alleged to have misbehaved, one can easily see how retaliation could occur. The issue is then always resolved in the corrections officer's favor because the investigator "failed" to find evidence supporting the offender's claims. What actions were taken to investigate the issue? The almost certain answer to such questions is an easy one: none whatsoever. Even the Grand Canyon can be missed if one never goes looking for it.

The 2008 audit also showed that 55 percent of inmates claimed they'd never been informed of the grievance program's existence.[5] Seventy-eight percent said they did not personally trust the grievance investigators.[6] Only one in twenty grievances was resolved through the process, with some minimal action taken. When it comes to the most sensitive grievances, those detailing some sort of threat or life endangerment claim, nearly 50 percent contained no documentation showing that appropriate staff had been alerted to the allegations—and by "appropriate staff," I mean literally anyone.[7] Almost one in three was not resolved within statutory deadlines. Out of 187 audited medical-related grievances, 13 did not have proper documentation showing an investigation even took place, and 4 could not be found at all.[8] Despite this Category 5 shitstorm of incompetence, the authors of the report go out of their way to praise the program, stating:

> The Department of Criminal Justice substantially complies with its policies and procedures relating to investigating and resolving offender and employee grievances, investigating complaints, and processing allegations of policy violations and criminal behavior.[9]

Only in government could a 78 percent disapproval rating be considered a passing mark. If anyone cares to sit through a lesson on how Texas GOP bureaucrats oversee themselves, this report is a masterpiece.

The second current layer of oversight is the Office of the Ombudsman, located in the same Risk Management Division as the grievance system. The principal function of this program is to act as a liaison between the public and the prison system. Depending on the concerns of the citizen contacting the office, the Ombudsman may answer questions regarding agency policies, procedures, or actions; make a referral to another office within the Texas corrections system; or act as an information source for what the office's own literature disdainfully refers to as "special interest groups." All that is well and good; as always, however, the devil is in the details, and thanks to activists and their annoying proficiency with the Texas Open Records Act, we have plenty of this particular devil's details.

House Bill 1 of the General Appropriations Act, Article V, Rider 51, requires that the Ombudsman's Office provide annual reports on the number and types of inquiries made by the public; for the report generated for the state's 84th Legislature, this figure totaled 35,374 calls between September 1, 2016, and August 31, 2017.[10] And what a report it is. The first thing to note about this behemoth is that it was produced by either a wizard of statistical legerdemain or an absolute lunatic; my money (no more than a few bucks) is on the former. I suspect that whoever generated this wilderness of funhouse mirrors was very aware that there are few things conservative politicians care less about than the daily nuts-and-bolts operations of the prison system. Because the office was mandated to produce the audit, it did so, but it carved the data up into so many categories (nineteen), sub-fields (between ten and twenty-nine per category), and sub-sub-fields (several hundred in total, or twenty-four pages' worth), that one practically needs a degree in forensic accounting to keep sight of the forest for the trees.[11] In short, the office knew perfectly well that no one was going to spend the requisite hours needed to decipher this record. Fortunately, or unfortunately—one wrestles with the choice of adverb—I have no life.

The "Classification" category, for instance, contains thirteen subfields, ranging from "Housing/Unit Assignment" to "Time Calculations"; unpacking these further reveals fifteen and seven additional subfields, respectively. While each of these lower-level fields is unique to their parent categories, each contains similarities that are universal throughout the report. In every single subfield, a single field dominates the statistics: "General information provided/Policy or procedure explained." In the "Housing" subfield, this field accounted for 970 of 1,464 (66 percent) of the inquiries; in "Time Calculation," it accounted for 188 of 235 (80 percent).What this designation actually means, once translated out of bureaucratese and into regular English, is that an inmate had a problem, then shared this difficulty with family or friends in the free world, and that representative contacted the Ombudsman. Once on the line, that representative had policy thrown in their face. Understand what this does *not* mean: it does not signify that an investigation was ever conducted. Neither does it confirm that any action was taken to rectify the problem—indeed, it points to the exact opposite outcome, that the caller's complaint was deemed meritless or outside the scope of the Ombudsman to address: This is the policy, now y'all have a nice day.

The situation gets worse when you recognize that nearly all the other subfields are essentially different ways of saying "no action taken." This is easy to miss—look at all the words!—but "requested additional information" and "offender information provided" all effectively mean, "go away and stop bothering the Department." Once you separate the signal from the noise, the near-irrelevance of the Ombudsman becomes clear: only 48 of 1,464 (3 percent) of classification inquiries and 1 of 235 (0.4 percent) of time-calculation inquiries resulted in some genuine change in the life of the prisoners involved. This program is to the ideals of due process what a discarded plastic saint is to God: the cheapest of idols, pointing not to the entity it symbolizes but to its exact antithesis.

The Office of the Inspector General is the third layer of oversight in Texas prisons. This office serves as the primary law enforcement and investigative entity within the Texas Department of Criminal Justice. Unlike the Risk Management Division, the office stands somewhat to the side of the rest of the department's hierarchy, with the inspector general serving by appointment by the Texas Board of Criminal Justice. There's very little I can say from personal experience about the OIG because I've never actually seen anyone from that office in my fourteen years behind bars. I've heard stories about them in the media, but I've never personally witnessed a single corrections officer investigated by the Office of the Inspector General for anything—not for beatings, not for the river of narcotics inundating these facilities, not for any of a thousand daily occurrences where a corrections officer invents policy on the spot to justify laziness or ineptitude.

And why would they? All these people—the grievance officers, the corrections officers, the inspectors—live in the same small rural communities. They go to the same bars, the same churches, their children play on the same sports teams. Often they are married to officers: three of the five grievance officers at my last unit were spouses of current corrections officers. Of perhaps more importance is the fact that all five *were* former corrections officers. Imagine for a moment what it would be like for them, were any of these oversight employees to suddenly begin to aim for some degree of true impartiality. They would quickly be labeled as being "friendly" to inmates, a slur in this world that has no direct analogue to anything from yours. They would inevitably become ostracized from their community. Who among us would be willing to live the life of an outsider for the sake of an unruly pack of inmates, all for a measly thirty grand a year?

A recent incident at the Ramsey Unit, a prison facility in Rosharon, highlights both the chummy relations within these oversight programs as well as their cumulative inefficacy. During the closing months of 2017, inmates began to file grievances alleging the existence of a quota system for disciplinary cases. These were all denied, supposedly after an investigation failed to find supporting proof. Multiple families sought an answer from the Ombudsman, who told them that policy did not permit the existence of such quota systems. Of course it doesn't: quota systems, just like all policy violations, are not permitted by policy to exist. That's what makes them a violation in the first place. This says nothing about whether they do in fact ontologically exist, however. Watch the wordplay here. In logic, this is an example of a species of fallacy known as an *ignoratio elenchi*, in which someone supposes to refute an argument by disproving something that was not actually asserted. It seems to be something of a favorite with the Ombudsman.

This is the point where, after having run face-first into a wall of institutional indifference at Mach 7 speed, most inmates give up. Instead, the cons at Ramsey Unit got clever, somehow managing to obtain and then smuggle past the razor wire internal documents showing the parameters of an alleged quota system instituted by Captain Reginald Gilbert and approved of by Major Juan Jackson.[12] This documentation was then sent to the *Houston Chronicle*, which ultimately attracted the attention of Senator John Whitmire, chairman of the Texas Senate Criminal Justice Committee.

"Every time I think I've seen everything, I see this . . . it's nuts," concluded Whitmire. Responding to the *Chronicle*, Jeremy Desel, the Texas Department of Criminal Justice spokesman, said, "This incident is the result of the action of one unit captain, which was quickly discovered and corrected by the unit warden."[13] But the subsequent investigation, initiated by Senator Whitmire, revealed three other quota systems at the first three units they inspected. Whoops. Suddenly the "one rogue captain" theory was beginning to look a little suspect.

Pause for a moment to take note of all of the unlikely events that had to add up in just the right way for the prisoners' grievance allegations to be proven. Convicts managed to work together to scheme a way to obtain the evidence from the department's mainframe; said evidence had to then get successfully smuggled past the mailroom screeners and into the hands of capable citizens; there had to exist a politician who still somehow possessed a moral conscience, a desire to get involved, and a working knowledge of how the Texas justice system operates; and a group of inspectors had to be willing to tell the truth about the other quota systems found. That's quite a collection of low-probability events adding up to something that looks like genuine review. How often do you think all of those stars align?

I think the dimensions of the problem are more or less clear by this point. I have read several dozen white papers over the years detailing potential solutions to prison's oversight problem. Nearly all of these involve the importation of robust monitoring regimes from international jurisdictions that are vastly more progressive than most states in this country, especially Texas. Barring a surprise invasion by the Swedish military, these plans are mere forays into delusion. Six different advocacy groups have distributed calls for the United States to ratify the Optional Protocol to the Convention Against Torture and Other Cruel, Inhuman or Degrading Treatment (OPCAT), a United Nations treaty that requires the creation of a network of independent oversight bodies.[14]

Enough with the fantasy: that is simply not going to happen. Not in a state where significant numbers of conservative evangelicals seriously believe the UN to be somehow connected to the rise of the Antichrist. This sad truth was on full display a number of summers ago, when a planned U.S.

military exercise in central Texas involving UN strategists so riled up the far right that Governor Greg Abbott actually called up the Texas National Guard to monitor the Army's activities.[15] Any proposal involving international law or international norms simply isn't worth the paper it is printed on. Think smaller.

Likewise, any plan that involves either the firing of large numbers of current employees of the Texas Department of Criminal Justice or the creation of a significant new government bureaucracy is similarly a nonstarter. This includes the creation of an independent grievance office, an idea that has been floating around in the blathersphere for ages. Consider what this would require: the firing or reassignment of roughly a thousand current employees of the department, the hiring of an equal number of currently non-aligned personnel, and the creation of an agency in Austin to coordinate the actions and policies of these new employees. Who would take these jobs? Texas prison positions do not pay well—this is why so many COs sell narcotics to inmates. Each position would require someone to relocate to rural Texas, where, eventually, they would be labeled as outsiders by the rest of the unit's employees or else fall into the same chummy relationship with the officers as their predecessors had.

Similarly, I am skeptical that detaching the Ombudsman's Office from the department would prove effective, although this shift would certainly cost less than gutting the grievance program. State Representative Jarvis Johnson and State Senator Borris Miles filed a bill to do just this in 2017, though the bill failed before a vote in the Republican-dominated House; they intend to file this bill again during the 2019 session, as far as I know.[16] The principal problem with their idea is that they would move the Ombudsman under the purview of the Texas Commission on Jail Standards, a body overseen by a board that is appointed by the governor. Since the Board of Criminal Justice is also appointed by the governor, one cannot help but wonder just how effective this move would end up being. What would prevent the governor from appointing members whose core ideologies run exactly contrary to those hoping for reform? If this sounds like some kind of conspiracy theory, I suggest you research the ways that this very thing happened after the creation of the state's Forensic Science Commission. In any case, the Texas Commission on Jail Standards has authority over county jails, not the state prison system. Even if the bill somehow magically corrected these two flaws, let us not lose sight of the fact that the Ombudsman has zero power to change policy in the department. At best, they might be able to resolve a few more problems than they can at the moment—a pleasant outcome, no doubt, but hardly the sort of change that we prisoners are, on occasion, literally dying for.

I have been thinking about this problem for some time. Many of my more realist contacts in the reform community have become so discouraged by the political realities of this state that they have basically abandoned specific proposals in favor of vague promises of a demographic time bomb that will supposedly explode one day, ushering in a legislature more open to changes. These people might be right, though this conclusion isn't particularly helpful. Despite everything I've written, I do think that there might be two minor structural weaknesses in the Texas Department of Criminal

Justice's armor that could be exploited to produce some modest gains. The first is a simple point that nonetheless tends to get ignored in the rampant demagoguery that dominates our political discourse these days: the majority Republican legislature isn't ignorant of the problems inside the TDCJ. They are very aware that they have created a system that costs billions of dollars ($3.6 billion was requested for fiscal year 2019), regularly kills people (6,913 human beings died in Texas in custody between 2005 and 2015), and virtually guarantees recidivism.[17] During biennial funding hearings, legislators regularly complain that the department seems incapable of resolving problems until they have metastasized into massively complicated ones requiring mountains of funds. They're not happy with the state of our prison system, but as a group they tend to think government is responsible for every human evil since The Fall, and they know that their base will not approve of the creation of a new government agency—especially one intending to benefit prisoners. They aren't completely hostile to the concept of reform, they just want these changes to be managed by as few people as possible and for minimal cost.

They also want any reforms to be handled by individuals who are ideologically in line with themselves and their constituencies. Here we find the second point of vulnerability that could potentially be utilized for our purposes, one that takes advantage of a certain inconsistency—or, more aptly, "hypocrisy"—in the way conservative Christians view prisoners, punishment, and crime. The root of this difference lies in the discrepancy found between the Old Testament's harsh treatment of malefactors and what is found in the New Testament, and the various theological structures that have been developed over the centuries to rationalize this incongruity.

A model known as Penal Substitution is currently in vogue with Neo-Calvinist churches, which we have in abundance in Texas (many of which belong to the Southern Baptist Convention) and which make up the most powerful voting bloc in the Republican primary process in this state. The central precept of this model emphasizes the terrible nature of sin and how an angry deity has to be propitiated. In theological terms, the sacrifice of Jesus was meant to satisfy this stain; in practical, earthly terms, however, groups that follow this framework (for example, the Puritans) have always sanctioned draconian punishments for trespass in the here and now. One doesn't have to travel very far down my radio dial to locate preachers railing about the "permissive" society in which we live, and the need for a return of "the rod."

The other side of that coin can be found in the abundant passages in a number of the synoptic Gospels (not to mention a few choice passages in Hebrews) that clearly require Christians to care for prisoners. A number of both liberal and conservative church groups do this very thing, holding revival ceremonies in prison gymnasiums all across the state. Indeed, these groups are the only non-essential, non-security-related human beings ever permitted to enter Texas prisons. Prison administrators are clearly divided on the issue, but there are enough co-religionists within the higher echelons of the criminal justice bureaucracy and the Texas legislature that such events have been regular occurrences for decades.

And these people have power. For example, in order for their video equipment to operate, all radio traffic between officers must be curtailed. In all of my time behind bars, the only times I have ever seen the authorities shut down the hand-held radios are during these rallies. They even let groups of these evangelists back into the ad-seg wings, something that isn't permitted much among the prison's own mental health personnel. I have spoken to a number of these volunteers over the years. They all desire to have an increased presence in the prisons; one told me he'd prefer to make monthly trips. To another inmate, they also admitted to being appalled by the conditions they witnessed. Here, we have a ready group of observers with access, people already approved by the conservative establishment to pass through the otherwise impermeable membrane of the prison. The question then becomes how to take their desire to help and mold it into an effective monitoring mechanism.

The model that comes closest to being the right puzzle-piece shape can be found in the United Kingdom. Since the 1950s, Independent Monitoring Boards (IMBs) have operated in every detention center in the nation. Board members are unpaid volunteers, living in the communities around each prison facility, who agree to conduct inspections and then write reports that are submitted to local politicians and prison administrators.[18] On average, each institution has around a dozen volunteers assigned to it, and each tends to conduct three to four visits per month—a considerable presence, nearly constant. While inside the prisons, IMB members can speak to prisoners, inspect kitchen facilities, and attend disciplinary hearings. The reports they generate are remarkably detailed, especially considering these citizens have zero formal training in prison administration.

It is unlikely that an exact replica of the British system could exist here in Texas, but as a model, there is much to be said for any attempt to approximate it. The cost of such a program would be minimal: the actual inspectors would be volunteers, so the only public funds needed to create the regime would likely be for the salaries of a few people in Austin tasked with collecting the various reports and summarizing the results for the legislature. No one currently employed would lose their jobs. Most importantly, the people making the pitch would be the most valued constituents of the most important legislators in the state.

Once such a program is framed correctly, explaining its value to legislators is not actually as difficult as one might expect. In a state dominated by fiscal conservatives, the central argument in favor of reform should always be that it will *save money*. Instead of allowing problems to fester so long that heavy funding is required to resolve them, the monitors could identify legitimate issues early in the process, make suggestions on optimal solutions, and forward this data to administrators above the level of unit warden. This last point is important, because there is a boundary along which the principal concern of administrators changes from security—the art of making nothing happen—to cost-effectiveness—the need to make things happen in specific ways. This demarcation exists somewhere between the unit warden and the regional director. The current oversight regimes exist entirely under the responsibility of the unit wardens, for whom fiscal concerns are relatively minor, and thus they will always instinctively prioritize solutions that promise to buttress the way things have always been done. This point, while remarkably uncomplicated, has simply not been understood by any of the groups currently debating policy changes. You have to bypass the wardens: they are not our friends in this business.

There is also a security component to this argument. At the moment, prisoners confronted with a legitimate problem have only other prisoners and hostile grievance officers to engage with. This breeds an environment where one's frustration level slowly ratchets up to a full boil. When this happens, violence tends to erupt. All I have to do is look around me to confirm this: inmates stabbing each other, launching spears out of improvised crossbows, using paint thinner to make homemade flamethrowers, Extraction Teams running daily. We all know how empowering it is to have another human to talk to about our problems; people pay huge sums of money to therapists for this very experience. Having monitors inside the units recording the complaints of offenders could have a major impact on the behavior of even the most incorrigible prisoners. Even if a problem cannot be resolved in the manner desired, if the inmate believes that a truly impartial arbiter is involved, it gives them an opportunity to get over their initial anger and move into a calmer headspace. Power corrupts, but so too does powerlessness. This system would inoculate against that feeling of impotency, helping to vaccinate offenders against anger and cynicism. This program has great potential to de-escalate a vast number of conflicts, leading to a safer environment for inmates and staff.

It would be an obvious win for human rights reasons, but it also promises even more financial savings.

There is a component of public safety here as well. Try to imagine what it would be like to live in an environment where every single contact one has with authorities is either adversarial, dishonest, or some volatile mixture of the two, and then what it would be like for those feelings to stretch over the length of even a short sentence. Now ask yourself what your reflexive response would be to any authority figures you encounter once you are released. Why would you trust the police or your elected officials? Why would you respect or adhere to any of the laws they promote and enforce? Why would you care about the citizens who follow those laws?

We all understand on some level that the high recidivism numbers we see in the United States are due in part to the prison environment itself. The punditocracy claims this is because criminals learn new techniques from their comrades, but I've honestly never seen one inmate sit down with another for the purposes of instructing them on how to commit crimes—not once in fourteen years. What prison does is grant criminals the will to commit new crimes. The mechanism behind this sorry reality is very simple: prison teaches all of us that America—its laws, its people, its culture, its values—hates us, the inmates, and that we will always be "othered" outsiders.

While it would be absurd to argue that introducing something like an independent monitoring board would totally solve this problem, I am not certain a civilian who has never set one foot into a prison wing could ever completely understand just how important it would be to introduce in this often contentious environment a third category to the for-us/against-us dichotomy. If reducing crime levels is an important goal to you, it might benefit you greatly to give this paragraph some additional thought. When you attempt to spell justice as W-A-R, nobody wins.

I suspect that some of my progressive friends would scoff at this plan. Monitors aren't a sexy concept. They wouldn't have much power, and the legislature would almost certainly neuter the few mechanisms contained in the United Kingdom's version that allow for changes in policy. But most civilian activists remain woefully ignorant about the actual state of our prisons, or what tools we need to improve them. They seem to have made a practice of letting the perfect become the enemy of the good.

As someone who is known to occasionally lob a lawsuit into the penal machinery, for me, the central problem has always been an inability to establish the corpus of facts necessary to prove my allegations. While some pro-prisoner changes in the judicial landscape would be lovely, I do not need any revolutions to win—I need a hidden camera system. Since such a piece of contraband is unlikely to come my way any time soon, I need the next best thing: a witness who has not been indoctrinated into the Texas Criminal Justice Department's dominant ethos, someone capable of saying, "Why yes, what this man says is true, is fact." What I need is a knowledge-gathering institution behind the walls, and the system I have described above is the only one I can envision that has even a tiny chance of leaping from the pages of theory into the world of reality. Were we given such a breach in the razor wire, a tiny ray of light that would make our reality visible to the broader society's gaze, I and many other writers would be empowered to flood our courts with cases that could help us drag our backward criminal justice system into the twenty-first century.

You might notice that my dilemma is akin to what progressive America is being forced to confront in the Trump era. How does one prove that any figure in power is lying to you? What is one to do when living in a climate where no fact, event, or aspect of history has any fixed meaning or content? You, however, have the media, statutory checks and balances, citizen watchdogs, and, ultimately, the ballot box to combat the desires of such people. I have none of that. Make no mistake, though: we are fighting the same enemy. The people who run this prison system are the same people banging the war drums for their side of the *Trumpenkulturkampf.* For those of you worried about the country sliding into fascism or totalitarianism, here's a sobering bite of reality: I already live in that America, and I can tell you that the only weapon we have in our arsenal is facts. Without the ability to gather truthful information or even have the existence of such facts confirmed, you are done for. Without oversight, your world becomes my world.

3

Unlock Digital Inclusion

Teresa Y. Hodge

Teresa Y. Hodge is the co-founder and CEO of R3 Score Technologies, Inc. and is committed to reducing the harm prison causes to individuals and their families. After completing a seventy-month federal prison sentence, she co-founded Mission: Launch, Inc. with her daughter Laurin Leonard. Hodge is a Technology and Human Rights Fellow at the Carr Center for Human Rights Policy at the Harvard Kennedy School. Previously Hodge was an Echoing Green Fellow and a Soros Justice Advocacy Fellow, and is an alumna of JustLeadershipUSA's inaugural Leading with Convictions cohort. She proposes access to high-speed internet and digital literacy resources for incarcerated people.

I arrived in prison January 3, 2007. Six days later, Steve Jobs, the founder of Apple, stood on a stage and presented the device that would change the world. He called it a 3-in-1 product: "a widescreen iPod with touch controls, a revolutionary mobile phone and a breakthrough internet communications device."[1] He was correct; the device, the first-generation iPhone, changed everything. Over the next few years, social media and technological advances forever changed the digital connectedness of the world. But for those of us incarcerated, the digital divide grew wider. I sat in prison with a sinking feeling, knowing that technology was transforming the world while I was being left behind.

While serving time in federal prison, I had little-to-no access to technology, which made engaging with my family and the outside world at large beyond challenging. Reading about social media, seeing the surge in blogging, and learning about the rise of smart phones while incarcerated was the first time I experienced the digital divide as an American. Before my incarceration, I was an early adopter of technology; I often spoke about the importance of learning computer skills, purchased the latest devices and software for my daughter, and insisted that she learn and use technology whenever and wherever possible.

I vowed to come home and once again become digitally literate. I have always felt a great pang for the women and men in prison who might not have seen the technology transformation as I did, and would not be as intentional as I was about including technology in their reintegration strategy. I also knew that many might not have the support systems and resources I had upon release to make technology a part of their life post-incarceration.

The day I was released from prison, my daughter handed me her iPhone 4. Laurin loves technology (probably because I was such an advocate), so it was no surprise that she would have the latest version of the iPhone and an iPad with her the day she arrived to pick me up. I read about the advances in tech but honestly didn't really process that I was four generations delayed in my exposure to the device until I first touched it and attempted to use it. I naively assumed it would be easy to pick back up where I left off as a consumer of tech. I was wrong. Laurin's phone was my portal to receive the phone calls and text messages from family members and friends who wanted to send their well-wishes. So while I was excited to reconnect with my loved ones and was thrilled to hold an iPhone, other feelings were rising to the surface: frustration, anxiety, and a sense of being overwhelmed. I was discouraged that I couldn't seem to figure out how to use the device I had read so much about while incarcerated. After twenty minutes of fumbling around, I handed the phone back to my daughter and told her, "Just tell them I said hello and thank you."

What follows is my perspective on how digital inclusion for individuals living with criminal records should be prioritized for those in the U.S. exiting prison or jail. If successful reentry is about social integration, and our society is dependent on technology, we must ensure that individuals are given the skills, tools, and opportunities upon their return to become "plugged-in," productive members of our technology-reliant society.

A Manifesto of Radical Inclusion

Technology is an accelerant. Over the course of recent history and across the globe, we can trace many advancements in economic mobility and social standing to access to internet, digital literacy training, hardware, and software.

In the United States, where one in three Americans has a criminal record, we must address the economic realities and hardships that accompany such a high rate of incarceration.[2] Our nation's economy cannot sustain the costs of the criminal justice system, nor can those who have to deal with the forty thousand–plus barriers to successfully rejoining society.[3] These collateral consequences affect not only one's ability to earn a livable wage, but also to find housing, pursue education, access banking and financial products, and reconnect with family and community, as well as enter any proven pathway out of poverty.[4] In effect, we have one-third of our population that, though no longer incarcerated, is forever at risk of being locked out of opportunity if we don't radically intervene.

Across this country, we are now seeing many formerly incarcerated tech founders changing the trajectory of their lives through tech-enabled solutions and serving as reformers in the criminal justice movement.[5] Let's not make them the exception to the rule. Instead, let's invest in them and base scalable solutions on their models. Let's not take half-measured solutions; let's get aggressive about unlocking inclusion. Let's not focus on teaching those with criminal justice-involvement basic tech skills; let's advocate for the kind of digital inclusion that empowers directly affected individuals to create the tech themselves.

The readily available data consistently show that digital inclusion offers a pipeline for increasing equality and creating opportunities.[6] Therefore, the digital divide that only widens when individuals are stripped of technology during incarceration can be closed up by increasing access to such opportunities post-incarceration and working to find ways to keep inmates from losing connection to tech while in prison. Some institutions are already working to bridge the divide by allowing incarcerated individuals to use mobile tablets with a form of intranet, and hosting coding and basic digital literacy courses.[7] While these measures are a step in the right direction, they are not uniformly available and are not enough in and of themselves.

What Radical Inclusion Looks Like

Ensuring that people living with criminal records are included in the digital movement is going to take radical effort—the kind of effort that has the power to shift our values, practices, and ultimately our outcomes. What I am proposing we do contradicts our fundamental beliefs about what incarceration should and could look like.

For example, when we examine the U.S. criminal justice system and the effects of mass incarceration, we can see the great lengths the system has taken to limit one's digital engagement, even as over 95 percent of people will come home to a tech-dependent society.[8] Many of these limitations stem from a concern about safety, as is illustrated in "Using Technology to Make Prisons and Jails Safer," an article published by the National Institute of Justice that argues for the expansion of efforts to keep people from using certain technology as well as phones in the commission of harmful acts.[9] While this makes some sense, it continues to reinforce the notion that technology is dangerous and that certain people would become more dangerous with access to technology. Notably, the criminal justice system is not wholly averse to using technology; in fact, there is a growing move to use data in a punitive and harmful manner to prop up our "incarceration nation" status. Movements toward dangerously biased algorithms, expensive video calls in place of visitation, and hardware that can extend the reach of our supervisory institutions into homes are already gaining traction. This is not what I mean by "radical inclusion of tech."

The radical inclusion I am advocating for requires rigor to strike a balance. We must do what we can to keep each other safe, but we also absolutely must challenge tech and data advances that are harmful and could set back justice reform efforts. In doing so, we can't tire of finding smart ways to ensure that prisons and jails are not isolating people from tech. We also can't lose sight of growing movements that position technology as a global human right. Some of the nation's leading thinkers have begun discussing what it means to have the internet as a right, and how artificial intelligence affects the protection of that right. When these conversations occur, criminal justice and those affected by mass incarceration cannot be an afterthought. Already, we see examples of humans coding their bias into algorithms that impact bail, sentencing, and even "e-carceration." In a world where fewer and fewer humans will be making decisions in general, it is critical that we address how AI will impact the people with criminal records.

Ten Steps to Unlock Inclusion

If we are to "unlock inclusion" by harnessing the power of technology in reentry, we need to anchor ourselves to some actionable steps. I offer these ten steps as a starting point for discussion:

1. *Ensure access to high-speed internet.* Globally, we have observed that education, employment, and even health can improve en masse with universal internet access.[10] Being able to search the internet with ease levels the playing field.

2. *Increase access to hardware.* The digital world shapes so much of our everyday experience. Access to the physical tools of tech (such as phones, tablets, data storage units, modems, and computers) is a foundational priority for our incarcerated and formerly incarcerated citizens.

3. *Support digital literacy learning communities.* For many, the burden of digital literacy feels too heavy, but learning with others brings down barriers to comprehension.

4. *Promote tech industry courses and certifications.* Tech industry professional certifications can provide pathways into lucrative careers while bypassing traditional barriers to occupational licenses and higher education.[11]

5. *Establish fair chance hiring practices.* We know that nine in ten employers run a criminal background check.[12] But background checks were designed for use by law

enforcement to investigate crimes, not for use by human resource departments to assess workplace readiness. This is the wrong tool for hiring for several reasons, so we must endeavor to find more appropriate ways to address an employer's safety concerns outside of the standard background check, which can't really assess someone's suitability for a job.

6. *Credit solutions built by directly affected individuals.* As the market need becomes more obvious, we see people of privilege "picking the brains" of individuals living with convictions. This exploitative practice must end. When solutions built by tech leaders who happen to have records become a priority, we will see unique opportunities for this population to receive funding and training in app and other product development.

7. *Remove cultures of stigma and shame.* A key way to reduce the incapacity that often accompanies having a record is speaking more about America's over-incarceration crisis in public and private gatherings. When we fully acknowledge that one-third of our population is justice-involved, we allow millions of Americans to show up, without having to deny their lived experiences.

8. *Use humanizing language.* Using discriminatory labels like "ex-con" and "ex-felon" keeps a person locked into their worst mistake and paves the way for significant inequality.[13] In the absence of such stigmatizing language, we will more effectively work together in finding solutions that promote equity and equality.

9. *Establish a strategic capital fund.* Community and na-

tional foundations must work together with the private sector to build up the resources required to invest in direct services, systems interventions, ecosystem building, innovations, and untried concepts, as well as tech infrastructure for communities in need.

10. *Divest from prison labor, invest in reform.* Across the country, corporations are able to secure a grossly underpaid workforce by hiring individuals in prisons or jails.[14] Exclusively pursuing a bottom-line outcome by participating in this practice does not help the U.S. economy. Instead, corporations should look to create real jobs in the open market for workers with records and, again, especially workers in the tech and digital sectors. Those who have already engaged in these exploitative practices should endeavor to convert incarcerated work history into transferable jobs upon release.

Conclusion

For millions of individuals living with their convictions, the role of an individualized reentry plan and access to the building blocks of life (such as a livable wage, safe housing, a supportive community, and reliable transportation) cannot be overestimated. As a society, we can hold people accountable for their actions, while also never losing sight of their humanity. Everyone deserves to know opportunity awaits them if they are willing to put in the effort. In today's world, finding and applying for critical opportunities upon reentry requires basic technology skills to navigate the internet and submit a competitive application package. I realize that tackling tech and digital engagement may not seem as urgent as other criminal justice issues, but I truly believe the interplay of tech in our daily lives can't be ignored. The first step we take may prove to be as simple as establishing tech as a reentry right, and aligning this core belief with our values, policies, processes, and practices. In doing so, we lay the groundwork for the courage we urgently need to face the future.

As a woman directly impacted by the criminal justice system and as an advocate for reentry and technology reforms, I often receive correspondence from currently and formerly incarcerated women and men. They write to me sharing the apps, websites, and products they too want to create. They are seeking guidance on how to become a tech founder, and often I am left unsure about how to continue to inspire them, knowing that an organized infrastructure of support and training is lacking for us.

As the discussion continues to grow about tech and criminal justice, prioritizing tech inclusion for people living with records could unearth funding resources to address the lack of infrastructure in this area. Being intentional about tapping into general interest in this issue could also help us invest in the human capital of people living with criminal convictions. Imagine a world where the leadership of the justice-involved in this field protected us from the human rights violations that no doubt await us in the coming years as we see further advances in automation, robotics, and other technology. Having skilled tech professionals with records means we don't have to figure out how to uncode bias, because someone who served time in prison might already be at the table to prevent such bias in the first place. This is our moment to correct the future *now.* The next big tech innovation is just waiting to be resourced and brought to market from the mind of an individual living with a record, if only we would unlock such a possibility.

4

On Prison Labor

Ty Evans

Ty Evans has published three self-help books on prisoner criminal litigation under his pen name Ivan Denison: Flipping Your Conviction *(2013),* Flipping Your Habe *(2014), and* The Essential Supreme Court Cases *(2015). His most recent publication is* Fifty Million Years in Prison: The Futility of Prisoners Seeking Justice in America *(2018), a nonfiction narrative account of prisoners fighting their cases post-conviction, exploring the causes of mass incarceration and what it would take to end it. He has two books ready for publication in 2020:* Religious Rights of Prisoners *and* Flipping your Guilty Plea. *Evans is a regular contributor to www.prisonwriters.com and is currently serving a seventy-one-year sentence in Indiana for attempted murder and resisting arrest.*

In 1983 my sentencing order committed me to ten years "at hard labor" in the Florida Department of Corrections. It wasn't an empty phrase; the hard labor definitely existed and was cast upon me, in the form of sling blade, shovel, sledgehammer, broom, mop, and kitchen duty. I received no financial compensation for over twelve thousand hours of work.

Forced labor without pay is the standard definition of slavery. The 13th Amendment to the U.S. Constitution specifically allows states to enslave prisoners. It didn't "abolish" slavery, as innumerable commentators have so carelessly repeated, but rather restricted slavery to prisoners "as a punishment for crime whereof the party shall have been duly convicted."[1] I was duly convicted, and I was effectively made a slave. I later learned that "hard labor" was a legal term of art, designed to insulate the state from any claims arising from my involuntary servitude.

The majority of people in America, and in the world, believe slavery is morally wrong. What need to be addressed are the perceptions that (1) prison labor does not qualify as "slavery," and (2) if it is slavery, it is a tolerable and necessary exception. To address those perceptions, it is necessary to re-examine why slavery is morally wrong in the first place, before extending the logic to situations that others may argue qualify as exceptions.

For over two thousand years, societies allowed slavery to be practiced under a philosophy best expressed by Aristotle, who said that slavery is "just" if it satisfies two conditions: (1) it is a "necessity," and (2) it affects only persons "naturally suited to it."[2] Put another way, Aristotle's approval of slavery depended on "who the slave is" and "what we need him for." This utilitarian view prevailed for several centuries, but was then challenged in the eighteenth century by Immanuel Kant, who argued that any effort to base morality on some particular interest or desire was doomed to fail, because any such principle "was bound to be always a conditioned one and could not possibly serve as a moral law."[3]

As contemporary philosopher Michael Sandel's analysis of Kant's writing points out, "we can't base the moral law on any particular interests, purposes, or ends, because then it would only be relative to the person whose ends they were."[4] Instead, one should "act in such a way that you always treat humanity, whether in your own person or in the person of any other, never simply as a means, but always at the same time as an end." There is a "duty of respect we owe to persons as rational beings, as bearers of humanity," and "it has nothing to do with who in particular the person may be."[5]

Slavery in any form, for any purpose, objectifies human beings, turning them into "tools" or "property" that serve only particular narrow interests. Slavery violates doctrines of universal human rights. The sentences prisoners receive are ends in themselves, not means of production for the benefit of the state. We imprison people, ostensibly, as a correctional measure, to improve the natures and conduct of those imprisoned. Those are the "ends" of the exercise, the moral purpose of incarceration.

To treat prisoners as chattel, extracting their labor for free because it sure is a nice perk for those who benefit from that labor, rests on Aristotle's flawed reasoning, and violates the principle of human dignity, which is founded on the notion that slavery is morally wrong without exception. To argue that prisoners are "naturally suited" to this condition of servitude only regresses us to an immoral, pre-Enlightenment age.

Some still say that prison labor does not constitute slavery.

But it does legally qualify as slavery, as has been specifically declared by numerous federal court decisions since 1865. In 1992, in *Vanskike v. Peters*, the court acknowledged that the 13th Amendment prohibited prisoners' claims under specific sections of the Fair Labor Standards Act of 1938, because they were not "employees" as defined by that statute due to their condition of involuntary servitude.[6] The fact that they were compensated with a small prison wage did not qualify them as employees because such pay is "by the grace of the state."[7] Indeed, in many states, overwhelmingly so in Southern states, most prisoners receive no wage at all.

A focus on the South is warranted. Throughout the nineteenth century, prisons were placed on state-purchased former plantations, merely transitioning from one form of slavery to another. Texas bought ten plantations between 1899 and 1918, converting them to prisons with far more brutal conditions than existed under antebellum laws.[8] Angola, in Louisiana, and Parchman Farm, in Mississippi, are two of the most notorious former plantations still in operation as prisons today.[9]

A recent case from 2017 is an instructive example regarding how the courts have ruled on prison slavery. In the ruling on the case of *Hammond v. Collier*, in which Texas prisoners had objected to the exploitation of their labor, the federal district court referred to a previous ruling in the Fifth Circuit, which emphasized that "inmates sentenced to incarceration cannot state a viable 13th Amendment claim if the prison system requires them to work."[10] Essentially, compelling an inmate to work without pay does not violate the Constitution even if the inmate is not specifically sentenced to hard labor.[11]

Inmates likewise do not have a basis for a claim under the Fair Labor Standards Act if they are forced to work without compensation.[12] Moreover, "the refusal to work, by a group or even a single inmate, presents a serious threat to the orderly functioning of a prison. Any unjustified refusal to follow the established work regime is an invitation to sanctions."[13]

The only redeeming feature of the above opinion is the admission that American prisons could not function without prisoner labor. The system rides on the backs of the incarcerated. The ability to create slaves out of law-breaking Americans is not just a hypothetical situation, as many Americans may believe, but an actual abuse that has been ongoing for over 150 years.

Naturally, critics point out that prisoners are relieved, by dint of their immurement behind prison walls, of the obligations to pay for food, rent, utilities, and the like, and therefore should consider those provisions as paid for by the taxpayers as part of their "pay" for labor. It is true that the costs of living are greatly reduced for a ward of the state (as is the standard of living), and that the majority of a free person's labor is devoured by the daily cost of living. Nevertheless, the prisoner, like the free person, deserves to enjoy some benefit of their labor. This is the state's justification for paying prisoners, even if it is far less than the minimum wage required for free persons. Nationwide, the average daily prison wage is around eighty-six cents.[14] To provide them nothing at all, goes the justification, is slavery. But to provide them with no meaningful compensation, little more than a few pennies per hour, is still clearly exploitative and tantamount to slavery.

Another argument for maintaining the status quo is that

prisoners are "paid" in good-time credits, which bring their release dates, and their freedom, closer. Good-time credits, however, are subjectively awarded. I worked twelve-hour days, sixty-hour weeks, at Copeland Road Prison in Florida in 1991, utilizing a sling blade while working alongside the well-named Alligator Alley, and was due to receive three days off my sentence if I never missed a day. However, on one occasion I was hit in the eye by flying debris, causing permanent damage, and missed work for a day and a half. The 246-hour month I worked accorded me zero time off my sentence, for lack of "officially" being a 264-hour month. I later transferred to Hendry Correctional Institution, in Immokalee, where I worked three hours a day, five days a week, as a GED instructor, and received the maximum twenty days per month off my release date.[15] The good-time awards throughout the state were extraordinarily arbitrary and not connected to the amount of labor, type of labor, or dangerousness of the work. The credits actually depended primarily upon whether the supervisor liked you or not, or whether he or she held some begrudging personal conviction that good-time credits should not be given in the first place.

The state is not the only benefactor of prison slavery. Private corporations have managed to weasel in as well. Corporations have cleverly obtained prison contracts by creating business models dependent upon slave labor. Aramark, based in Philadelphia, is one of the largest beneficiaries, with food service operations in dozens of prisons. Here at Indiana State Prison, Aramark works prisoners up to ninety hours a week and pays them nothing, at great benefit to their bottom line. The Indiana Department of Corrections (IDOC) picks up the tab for Aramark, paying the kitchen workers up to twenty-five cents an hour (no extra for overtime), thereby saving Aramark the $7.25-an-hour minimum wage burden. Then Aramark turns around and sells us an Angus burger for five dollars and fries for two dollars—one meal for twenty-eight hours of labor. In theory, prison industries are not supposed to unfairly compete with private enterprises, but they do. The competition is unavoidable, and it comes at the expense of subtracting over a million jobs from the American labor force.

The Ashurst-Sumners Act of 1935, which prohibited the interstate shipment of prisoner-made goods, was passed with the intention of combating the issue of unfair competition between the prison industries and private enterprises, but prison-made goods and services inevitably have an effect on interstate commerce.[16] I worked at the UNICOR sign factory at FCI Cumberland, Maryland, where we did over $10 million a year in sales, making signs for the military, national parks, courts, and various government buildings. Since our only clients, by law, were government agencies, the myth that no freeworld businesses were adversely affected was allowed to flourish.[17] Surely, had our prison labor not been used, those agencies would have had to contract with private companies, whose employees were guaranteed no less than the federal minimum wage, along with other benefits and protections.[18]

UNICOR is but one of many prison industries thriving from prison labor. Most states have such programs, and most offer a small pay scale, like UNICOR's (I earned twenty-three cents an hour), but payment is not universal. Notoriously egregious is Texas Correctional Industry, which pays prisoners nothing for their manufacture of mattresses, shoes, clothing, janitorial supplies, and furniture—items that obviously are also produced by private industry.[19]

The ubiquitous availability of prison slave labor alters the incentives of prisons and their employees. It fosters a perverse drive to keep lockup units at maximum capacity in order to maximize profits. As evidenced at length in Tara Herivel and Paul Wright's book *Prison Profiteers*, an alarming number of criminal justice personnel also have vested interests in for-profit prison enterprises, which they don't perceive as an ethical dilemma.[20] These incentives affect due process as well. Fairness in court proceedings becomes secondary when the state demands bodies to man its profit-making machines. It's fair to draw a parallel between this scheme and how the Soviet Union under Stalin manipulated its criminal justice system to create a labor force for state construction projects and to open Siberia to economic development.[21] We have more prisoners now than the Soviet Union ever did, and the list of private beneficiaries of mass incarceration in the United States adds a dimension to the human rights problem that the Soviet Union never faced.

To reform the prison labor situation requires, first, the conviction that prisoners should not be treated as slaves, but as future citizens, worthy of dignity and respect at the end of the correctional process. That their labor has value should be taught through example; and in so doing, prisoners may learn that others' labor, and the property derived from that labor, has value. What is needed is a "Prison Labor Standards Act."

As a prisoner who has served time since 1980, I have seen a number of abuses in which the state took unfair advantage of prisoner labor, besides the mere refusal to pay wages. Work shifts can be long, and assigned tasks can be dangerous. Fifteen-hour shifts are required of some prisoners at Indiana State Prison, in a facility where jobs are scarce and a majority of prisoners sit idle. Splitting the shifts in two would employ double the number of prisoners, which would especially benefit prisoners who otherwise endure solitary confinement.

Setting work-hour caps for prisoners at eight hours a day and forty hours a week would go a long way to expanding the number of non-idle prisoners, as well as increase the future employability of those prisoners, another goal the correctional system should try to achieve. If there are not enough prisoners vocationally qualified for the available jobs, then teach them.

A minimum wage is absolutely necessary; otherwise, states will skirt the slavery problem by paying a minuscule wage. Paying 10 percent of the federal minimum wage would ensure that pay scales approximately keep up with living costs. Prisoners have spending needs and face exorbitant costs like anyone else, more so for some goods and services. In my experience, a prisoner's eight hours of labor at a rate of 25 cents an hour equates to six Ramen noodle soups, or two ounces of generic coffee, or eight minutes of phone time. It takes twenty hours of labor to pay for one doctor visit, and twenty more hours to pay for a prescription. So yes, 10 percent of the minimum wage, which would be 72.5 cents per hour today, is more reasonable.

The state should also be restricted from going to the "back door" on a prisoner's wages and extracting "costs and fees" for various purposes. There should be a 25 percent cap on the proportion of wages the state is allowed to extract from a prisoner's wages to pay for legal fees, restitution, and other debts. If a prisoner owes court fees, for example, they should still be guaranteed the remaining 75 percent of their paycheck. In no case, no matter how many debts the prisoner holds, should more than 25 percent be deducted.

There also should be no disciplinary punishment for "refusal to work." In every state, a refusal to work can cause a disciplinary write-up, with sanctions ranging from loss of certain privileges all the way up to the eventual loss of all good-time credits. To punish a prisoner in any manner whatsoever for refusal to work is preconditioned on the premise that the prisoner is a slave, forced to work. Either slavery is impermissible, or a refusal to work is impermissible—the two cannot stand together.

In a system in which a Prison Labor Standards Act is in place, we must also anticipate the coercive pressure to perform "volunteer" work. Sly prison administrators would seize on the concept of so-called volunteer work to subrogate the eight-hour and forty-hour work limits along with the pay requirement. They could also offer other perks to volunteers, like that of getting a daily shower, or of not living in solitary confinement.

Work assignments should not be given as disciplinary punishments either, on the basis of the same principle.

The net cost for upping prisoners' pay to 10 percent of the federal minimum wage would be substantial, a fact that may, at first, give taxpayers and politicians pause. By my calculation, in a state like Indiana, it would add almost $20 million to the IDOC budget, nearly 3 percent of the $720 million allotted annually. However, there is a simple way to offset the costs:

reduce the prison population by 3 percent. That's as easy as closing only one prison. And if 3 percent of the national population of 2.2 million seems like a lot of prisoners, put it in the perspective that we need to release 80 percent to get back to a "normal" incarceration rate, one in line with the rest of the modern nations in the world. Or, one could also look through the proper end of the telescope and see that spending $20 million on prisoner work pay in Indiana gains the state $200 million worth of labor.

A growing faction calls for amending the 13th Amendment, redacting the line allowing prisoners to be slaves. Such revision is needed, but it would not be enough, by itself, to enjoin states from abusing prisoner labor, because a love of slavery dies hard, even in modern-day America. A Prison Labor Standards Act is the Congressional legislation required to stop the exploitation of prisoner labor. In fact, a Prison Labor Standards Act could be enacted without amending the Constitution.

What would the American prison system look like if laws were passed reforming prison labor? For one thing, states may quickly realize they don't need to lock up so many people. The incarceration rate would nosedive, saving taxpayers billions, far offsetting the costs of prison wages. Then we might get judges to issue opinions like this fictional one:

> The Fifth Circuit, applying the new laws, recently emphasized that "inmates sentenced to incarceration have a viable Thirteenth Amendment claim if the prison system requires them to work." *Johnson v. Ali*, 959 F.3d 317 (5th Cir. 2021). Compelling an

inmate to work without pay violates the Constitution even if the inmate is specifically sentenced to hard labor. *See Johnson v. Ali,* 959 F.3d 317, 318 (5th Cir. 2021); *Miss. Dep't of Corr. v. Murray,* 961 F.3d 1167 (5th Cir. 2021).

Inmates likewise have a basis for a claim under the Prison Labor Standards Act if they are worked without compensation. *Johnson v. Loving,* 955 F.3d 562, 563 (5th Cir. 2021). Moreover, "the refusal to work, by a group or even a single inmate, poses no threat to the orderly functioning of a prison, because operating a prison is the state's burden, not the inmate's. Any inmate's refusal to follow the established work regime is unpunishable. Any work performed is by the grace of the prisoner." *Evans v. Florida,* 960 F.2d 833, 837 (5th Cir. 2021).

5

Correcting Excessive Sentences
of Youthful Offenders

Aaron Striz

*Aaron Striz is originally from Magnolia, Texas. He was first incar-
cerated in 1997 when he robbed a convenience store as a juvenile.
While awaiting sentencing, he attempted to escape and in the process committed aggravated assault on two officers. Striz has been in
administrative segregation, or long-term solitary confinement, since
2001. He spends twenty-four hours a day in a five-by-nine-foot cell
and is in ongoing litigation against the state of Texas for his indefi-
nite confinement in "ad-seg." He dreams of getting out of prison,
obtaining a law degree, and working to change the system to help
people still inside. He proposes a specialized program to rehabilitate
and release individuals who were under the age of twenty at the time
of their offense and who have served twenty years or more of their
sentence.*

When I was seventeen years old, I robbed a convenience store
in a tiny rural town near my own. Prior to that, I had no felony

record. I was high on drugs and trying to get money for more drugs. I flashed a pistol, my friend and I took the money, and we ran. No shots were fired. Nobody was physically injured. We were captured a few days later and began the slow, grinding, unfamiliar journey through the criminal justice system.

I committed my crime on October 1, 1997, exactly one month after a new law in Texas that drastically limited potential for parole went into effect.[1] After refusing to accept the prosecutor's final plea offer of twenty-five years aggravated (minimum twelve and a half years before parole eligibility), I entered an "open plea" of guilty to allow the judge to sentence me. While awaiting sentencing, my codefendant and I were subjected to endless crude taunts and harassment from jailers and deputies about prison rape and what happens to young white boys in prison. Youth, fear, and ignorance are a dangerous combination. I proceeded to make the worst decision of my life: I escaped, assaulting two guards in the process. Neither was seriously injured, but they could have been. Within hours I was recaptured, stripped naked, and placed in an isolation cell where I was subjected to unending threats, taunts, and dehumanizing conditions until I was on the verge of suicide. After a month of such treatment I was so disoriented that when they pulled me out for court, I would've accepted anything just to get away from there.

On the morning of my court date, my attorney came to visit me at the jail for the first time in eleven months, only to tell me that there was nothing he could do to help me. He coerced me into signing a "plea bargain" for three concurrent aggravated life sentences, of which I must serve a minimum of thirty years before even being considered for parole at the age of forty-eight. What a bargain. And because of my escape and designation as a "security risk," since 2001, I've been in administrative segregation, a euphemism for long-term solitary confinement, with no prospect of release to general population in the near future and no access to educational or rehabilitative programming. (In fact, the Texas legislature passed a law in the '90s prohibiting access to educational and rehabilitative programs for prisoners in ad-seg . . . which is ironic, because these prisoners are the ones who would benefit the most from it!)[2] Thus, with no such programs available to me, there is a minuscule chance that the parole board would ever grant me parole, as they often look to a record of participation as proof of suitability for parole. This means there is a very distinct possibility that I will spend the remainder of my life in solitary confinement, all because of a couple very poor decisions made by a drug-addicted, terrified teenager.

Although the facts of my situation are unique, I am by no means the only individual in here with an excessive sentence disproportionate to the crimes I committed as a teenager. What rational purpose does it serve to keep me, or anyone convicted as a teenager, imprisoned until the age of fifty or beyond? Murder convictions are routinely pleaded out for much lesser sentences. There is no justification for such sentencing disparities. How is that equal justice under the law?

Prisons were never intended for the purpose of vengeance, retribution, or lifetime incarceration. A penitentiary, as the name implies, is a place for penance in the name of justice, to be rehabilitated and then restored to society, to sin no more.[3] The ultimate goal of criminal justice reform is to return to these principles, to drastically reduce the use of, and need for, incarceration. This process can begin with incremental policies that, step-by-step, are able to gain the broad consensus necessary for legislative approval. One way to begin this process is by addressing a population of prisoners that is often overlooked in this debate: youthful offenders with excessive sentences that are often disproportionate to their crimes.[4]

What is the purpose of incarcerating a juvenile, a teenager, for the majority of their adult lives, only to release them in their fifties or sixties with no work history or references, no savings, and often no support network because most of their family has died or forgotten about them? How do these individuals have any chance of becoming productive, contributing members of society when they lack basic life skills such as opening a bank account, paying bills, obtaining medical care or health insurance—or in some cases even knowing how to drive a car? This is a recipe for failure and recidivism.

The practice of excessively sentencing youthful offenders is rooted in a reactionary overcorrection at a point in the history of our criminal justice system. It started as a backlash against the "revolving door" parole systems of the 1980s, which was seen as the cause of the crack cocaine and gang violence epidemics of the '80s and '90s. Media sensationalism exacerbated the backlash, stoking public fears and leading to the politicization of these issues. The impact extended across the political and legal landscape: prosecutors began to seek much longer sentences across the board, judges and juries imposed longer sentences in an effort to compensate for the "revolving door" prison system, and politicians jockeyed for votes by claiming to be tougher on crime than their opponents, while legislators began changing laws to ensure that prisoners served a longer portion of their sentences. Meanwhile, parole boards became less likely to grant parole, especially as "tough on crime" governors appointed their political allies (also of the "tough on crime" persuasion) as parole board members. This confluence of events created a period during the '90s where irrationally excessive sentences were imposed upon criminals, often grossly disproportionate to their crimes.

The effects of these excessive sentences were dramatic. In Texas, for example, they eliminated the policy of "mandatory supervision release." Under mandatory supervision, a product of the old laws of the '70s and '80s, a prisoner could be eligible for release if they had a combination of good-time and work-time credits, along with time served equal to 25 percent of their sentence. The parole board would have no discretion over whether or not to grant parole. Thus, for a twenty-year sentence, it's possible a prisoner had to be released after only serving four or five years.[5]

However, after several high-profile cases in which prisoners who were released early went on to commit heinous crimes that provoked public outrage, Texas's legislature responded by severely limiting mandatory supervision while increasing the necessary amount of time served before parole eligibility. This development, coinciding with decreasing parole approval rates, meant that same twenty-year sentence would now result in a minimum of ten years served before eligibility, with no guarantee of parole approval, and often multiple denials.

In cases where prosecutors, judges, and juries may have imposed a twenty-year sentence, they were now imposing forty- or fifty-year sentences for the same crime, trying to ensure that felons would serve more time in prison while also "setting an example" to future felons (which research shows does not work).[6] Individuals would now serve twenty to twenty-five years before even becoming eligible for parole consideration, which was unlikely to be granted. This fueled the prison boom of the '90s that in turn led to the metastasizing of the prison industrial complex, which had a disproportionate impact on those most affected by the crack cocaine and gang violence epidemics: young Black and Latino males.[7]

I would like to propose the creation of a program I call 20/20. Under the terms of 20/20, anyone who commits a crime before the age of twenty and has served at least twenty years should be enrolled in a specially designed program that provides vocational training and rehabilitative services. Upon completion of this program, they would be granted parole. The program should also include a post-release period of intensive supervision with GPS monitoring and continued participation in a rehabilitative program.

The feasibility of such a program is clear if we consider the Texas Department of Criminal Justice's existing Serious and Violent Offender Reentry Initiative (SVORI), which is a six-month pre-parole program with an additional one-year period of continuing rehabilitation, GPS monitoring, and intensive supervision.[8] This program, and others like it in other states, could assist with successfully reintegrating prisoners into society. This framework for the 20/20 program already exists outside of prison, although the programming would be modified to include a mandatory vocational certification so that the prisoner has employable skills upon release, increasing their likelihood of successful reintegration.

Requiring that these offenders serve a minimum of twenty years ensures that they have "aged out" and matured beyond the sixteen-to-twenty-five age demographic most likely to commit crimes, and reached an age where their cognitive functions are fully developed. This also increases the likelihood that these individuals have matured out of the typical age range for gang activity or membership, which in many cases was a contributing factor in the behaviors that led to their crimes. Participation in the 20/20 Program should, in fact, require a full disassociation from any and all gang activity or membership.

One immediate impact of such a program is it would be a step toward reducing the prison population, thus lowering the taxpayer burden of keeping these individuals incarcerated. Instead, these individuals become contributing members of society who work and pay taxes, lending to a net revenue increase. And as a result, the state is no longer responsible for the long-term warehousing and care of these aging prisoners whose health care costs only increase with age.

Finally, tracking the success of this program can serve as proof of concept for similar programs that have a larger scope and include a broader range of prisoners and prison-diversionary programs; and demonstrate how such programming can reduce the financial burdens and human costs of mass incarceration. Such a program would provide a pathway with standardized criteria and expectations for individuals to earn a second chance at life, rather than merely sitting around waiting for parole eligibility and hoping to be among the arbitrarily approved few who receive it.

How can any reasonable person, whether a liberal prison-industrial-complex abolitionist or a law-and-order conservative who speaks of Christian compassion and forgiveness, say that more than twenty years in prison is the appropriate punishment for a crime committed by a teenager? At what point do you give them an opportunity to prove they are no longer that same person and have earned a second chance at life?

6

An Act to Increase
Voter Registration and Participation

Corey "Al-Ameen" Patterson

Corey Al-Ameen Patterson was born and raised in Boston, Massachusetts, and is currently serving a fifteen-years-to-life sentence that began in November 2009. Patterson is vice-chair of the African American Coalition Committee (AACC) at MCI-Norfolk. In an effort to restore the right to vote for all incarcerated people in Massachusetts, he coordinated a coalition of prisoner suffrage advocacy groups—including Emancipation Initiative, the Harvard Prison Divestment Campaign, and Families for Justice as Healing—to jointly push for prisoner suffrage via a 2020 ballot initiative. He is enrolled in the Boston University Prison Education Program and is expected to graduate with a bachelor's degree in Interdisciplinary Studies in Spring 2021. He is a practicing Muslim, married to a loving wife, and together they have a son. He proposes informing incarcerated people of their voting rights, providing absentee ballots to people in custody who are eligible to vote while awaiting trial, and pre-registering people about to reenter so that they can vote immediately after release.

Around seven weeks before the 2008 presidential election, I found myself in the back of a Suffolk County prisoner transport van headed to the Boston Municipal Court Department, Dorchester Division, to be arraigned on new criminal charges. Though I had bail money, it didn't matter. Because I was already out on bail, a new arrest gave the court full discretion to revoke the bail I previously posted and detain me, usually no longer than a period of sixty days. In routine fashion, as I expected, the judge took full advantage of this discretion and sat me down for the full two months. Come election night, the only silver lining was that my cell door was positioned directly in front of the television suspended from the wall in the recreation area. It was there, from behind the glass window on my cell door, I witnessed Barack Obama become the first black man to become president of the United States. Whenever I recall this (and I do quite often), I cannot help feeling ashamed that I lost my opportunity to cast a ballot for the country's first black president—especially as a black man myself. What makes looking back at this experience most painful is knowing now, as I did not know then, that I was legally still eligible to vote even while incarcerated.[1]

Fast forward ten years later, Massachusetts State Rep. Russell Holmes visited MCI-Norfolk, and sat in our African American Coalition Committee (AACC) board meeting.[2] After the meeting he was so impressed with the vision, solidarity, and professionalism of our group that he promised to file the legislation we planned to draft. The civic engagement department, headed by Derrick Washington, came up with the idea of proposing legislation that would make criminal detention facilities responsible for helping eligible voters in their custody obtain absentee ballots. As fate would have it I was assigned the task of drafting the legislative text. I had missed the chance to vote for Obama myself, but this was my chance to make a difference for many others who would otherwise have identical experiences in the future. This legislation would raise voter participation among incarcerated citizens, especially for those in pretrial detention centers, since these facilities house the highest number of eligible voters. In 2008 I was eligible to vote—I was twenty-one, a U.S. citizen, and a pretrial detainee yet to be convicted (actually I was never convicted in the case the judge revoked my bail on because the charges were eventually dismissed)—but I didn't know it. Think about all the incarcerated citizens nationwide who don't know they can vote. If all detention facilities were obligated by law to provide new detainees with knowledge about their voting rights during orientation and help them obtain absentee ballots, just as they are obligated to administer TB tests or flu shots, without a doubt most people would take advantage.

The legislation would also assign these facilities responsibility for initiating the restoration of voting rights by helping ineligible voters to preregister upon anticipation of their release. After the discharge of an offender, the jail or correctional facility would be mandated to notify the secretary of state, who would then add the registrant to the statewide registration database.[3] Preregistration would minimize the many responsibilities ex-offenders inevitably face upon their release, providing them some relief from the pressures attached to beginning a new life after years of confinement. If jails and correctional facilities were to embrace these responsibilities, states would see increases in voter registration and participation, and our democracy would be strengthened as a result.[4] States would also likely see a reduction in recidivism, since voter participation is statistically connected to lower rates of recidivism.[5]

Once I completed the draft bill I named it "An Act to Increase Voter Registration and Participation, and to Help Prevent Recidivism." I solicited feedback from my department as well as from elly kalfus, of the Emancipation Initiative and lead director of its Ballots Over Bars project. I revised the bill several times before I completed the final draft. On November 3, 2018, the AACC was honored with the rare opportunity to present several draft bills before two members of the Massachusetts Black and Latino Legislative Caucus, State Senator Sonia Chang-Diaz and State Representative Russell Holmes. Representative Holmes agreed to sponsor my bill and Senator Chang-Diaz agreed to sponsor parts of the bill I drafted. Since then, Holmes has taken the initiative to draft a bill called "An Act Increasing Voter Registration and Participation and to Help Prevent Recidivism," closely mirroring the one I wrote and proposed to him on behalf of the AACC. Both legislators have filed bills in the Massachusetts legislature (H.669 & S.329) that were inspired by "An Act to Increase Voter Registration and Participation, and to Help Prevent Recidivism." The MBLLC also agreed to include these bills to their top-fifteen priority legislation list.

Below is some of the text of "An Act Increasing Voter Registration and Participation and to Help Prevent Recidivism" filed by Representative Holmes:[6]

(1) Suffrage is the vanguard of civil rights and liberties and the cornerstone of democracy. It is both a fundamental right and a civic responsibility. Reinstating the right to suffrage fortifies our democracy by boosting voter turn-outs and helping ex-offenders upon their release to reintegrate into society. Voting is an essential part of reassuming the duties of full citizenship. Though Massachusetts recognizes these facts, Congress can do more to increase voter participation by protecting eligible voters while they are incarcerated. Congress can also do more to enhance voter registration among returning citizens and thereby help deter recidivism.

(2) Massachusetts residents incarcerated for felony convictions cannot vote in any elections in the state while incarcerated. As a result, approximately 8,234 people in Massachusetts are currently denied the right to vote.[7] Unfortunately the majority of these disfranchised citizens come from the same communities, diminishing the voting power of these communities. From 2015 to 2018, over 60 percent of those who received new criminal sentences were from just four counties: Suffolk, Essex, Middlesex and Hampden.[8]

(3) Massachusetts disproportionately incarcerates people of color as well, so while people of color make up 18.2 percent of the state's population, 58 percent (or 4,982) of people disfranchised in Massachusetts due to imprisonment are people of color.[9] People incarcerated in prison for reasons other than conviction, such as pretrial detention or civil commitments, are allowed to vote by absentee ballot.

(4) Maine and Vermont are the only states that allow all incarcerated citizens to vote.[10]

(5) Most of the approximately 9,800 people incarcerated in Massachusetts county jails and houses of correction can vote in all federal, state, and municipal elections by absentee ballot—as long as they are eighteen years of age or older, United States citizens and are not incarcerated for felony convictions or voter fraud.[11] However, many jails and houses of correction across the state do not help incarcerated people obtain absentee ballots, and in fact some give false information regarding their voting eligibility. Even when incarcerated people have the funds and knowledge to request an absentee ballot, some city and town clerks illegally reject these ballots, leaving incarcerated people with little recourse.

(6) Massachusetts is one of fourteen states that prohibit people from voting while incarcerated in prison but return the right to vote immediately

upon release, considered the least restrictive category of offender disfranchisement.[12] However, evidence suggests that many people assume they remain disfranchised upon release.

(7) Though it requires the cooperation of different government agencies, this bill would most directly affect the department of correction and houses of correction, leaving with them the responsibility of helping eligible voters in their custody obtain absentee ballots and helping ineligible voters get pre-registered upon anticipation of their release. Streamlining these processes will conserve government resources and save taxpayer dollars. This act will also require the secretary of state to train city and town clerks on the laws relevant to this act.

(8) A correctional facility shall be a designated agency for the registration of voters. Upon request, a correctional facility shall provide voter absentee ballot applications to eligible voters within the custody of the facility.

(9) As part of the release process leading to the discharge of a person who has been disfranchised because of a felony conviction, the correctional facility shall provide that person with a voter registration form and a declination form, and offer that person assistance in filling out the appropriate form.

(10) Prior to the expiration of a prisoner's term,

the superintendent or administrator of the state or county correctional facility shall, in writing, notify the prisoner whose term expires that his or her voting rights shall be restored upon discharge.

7

On Honor Yards

C.T. Mexica

C.T. Mexica has a doctorate in comparative literature (theory and criticism) from the University of Washington. He recently complet-ed a postdoctoral fellowship at Arizona State University's School of Social Transformation. C.T.'s research is centered on the literature of crime, confessions, and confinement and on the social theory of tragedy, transformation, and transition. C.T. is currently working on a literary memoir on intergenerational incarcerations and the demimonde of bonded males in the United States. He is a 2019–2020 PEN America Writing for Justice Fellow. C.T. proposes the creation of "honor yards" in correctional facilities in order to encourage a more authentically rehabilitative environment.

Upon arriving at the co-ed Echo Glen Children's Center, I was sent to their lockdown cottage for being labeled as non-compliant and recalcitrant. I was on the early side of thirteen and weighed no more than one hundred and twenty pounds. My homie, F—, was being processed into an open campus cottage, Chinook, and I was to go to the institution's lock-down cottage, Toutle. I was sent to the original Toutle and was there when it switched names and cottages with Copalis (the "mental" cottage). The cottages—an architectural design foreign to me—at this institution were named after state rivers, but their idyllic labeling belied their actual function: to confine and punish the youthful offenders who would later fill her adult institutions. This is one of the places where the cycle of habitual incarceration begins. I would later encounter many of these occupants at other institutions, especially those of us who were state-raised and penitentiary-bound. A few others would make their way to mental institutions. I know of at least three occupants from Toutle who were later committed to mental institutions. Many of us were also over-medicated with a variety of antidepressants, namely doxepin, which gave us a nightly high and extra snacks (a Jolly Rancher and boxed fruit juice). Toutle was my introduction into one of our chief rites of passage: getting sent up. In the absence of positive ritual initiations, it is another one of the initiation processes that we appropriate and create for ourselves. Getting sent up is a ritual of institutionalization for the state-raised. On the outs (what we called the streets) one often hears of one being sent up:

What's up with Smilón?

Damn, homie, he just got sent up.

To be sent up marks the beginning of our institutionalization, which is why the usage of the term "the outs" highlights our anticipation of incarceration. As youth, many of us already had little faith and investment in civil society and, as a result, some of us aspired to know incarceration. Most of our encounters with the state were adverse. There you go, adverse encounters with the state. And, if you're an indigenous man in this country your very existence in the United States is adversarial, hostile, and seditious. It does not matter if you are still tribal, or like the vast majority of us, detribalized. Who do you think the Founding Fathers had in mind when they mentioned "domestic Tranquility" in the preamble to the U.S. Constitution? You see, before there was a sea-to-shining-sea there was always the fear of savage, skulking Indians just beyond the next forest, the next mountain range, and the next plain. It fed, and continues to feed, some of their fears. And beyond each landscape, the settler-colonial lexicon expanded from forts-being-held and wagons-being-circled to build-the-wall chants. What, didn't they teach you that the last free americans were led by Geronimo who wasn't even american? The homie Val certainly reminds us of that. Geronimo and Cochise were hostiles. How can a non-american even be seditious? The last free americans. Thereafter, all indigenous people were born into captivity. Prisoners of war who continue to bear witness to the injustices that never leave us. Colonial cousins of black folks brought to our lands in captivity. Brown and black folks who are related by the colonial wound of indignity.

A few of us, the true-believers, were categorized as incorrigible, irredeemable, and inherently violent. And, if you are a thinker—an influencer—you will be subjected to arbitrary targeting by the security hawks of the institution. Our paper trail, or "points" based on crude algorithmic scores that aggregated our "risk" levels, ensured that we would be perpetually tracked into lockdown placements. As a result, I have always had a distrust for algorithms or any statistic that purports to define me. Their cooked stats do not overstand the imprisoned soul. Anyway, most of us would not benefit from the juvenile system's original rehabilitative orientation. No, we would spend our formative years in a more punitive, control model where we each had a room of our own. The previous generation had tiers, whereas my generation had pods. All of this certainly hastened feelings of being unwanted, unloved, and unimportant. In response, some of us abruptly ceased to be adolescents. Some of us became gravely serious, and a few of us began to fully commit ourselves to a self-apprenticeship in violence. Yeah, that's it: from children of violence to men of violence. None of that boys to men shit. There's no end of the road when Mikey hears the tractors pave new routes to new prisons. (Those were the causes we sought, ¿qué no?) We were to be confined and monitored by strangers. A bunch of little boy blues. As for me, institutionalization further enhanced my estrangement from civil society. It was never really traumatizing for me, though. Incarceration was what I anticipated and that anticipation was a commanding overture to my adaptability to my institutionalization.

The parallel existence of the institutionalized is highlighted by experiences that have their own premiums of distinguishing features. Our marks of pedigree are determined by placements in higher security levels. The higher the security level, the more respect and admiration you receive among your peers on both sides of the fences and walls. In being sent up, many of the resilient learn to become ruthless, whereas most of the inadaptable are increasingly culled, bruised, and brutalized. This is where the convict mindset germinates. In my world of bonded males (gang member and gangsters), Toutle was to prove a promising placement. My experiences with lockdown units began at Toutle and were hardening effects that steeled my heart with too much grit. In my experience, true grit is ruthlessly pragmatic and ought not to be romanticized, especially among youths, as there are fewer things that are more dangerous than the zealousness of youth.

As much as a cottage can be a lockdown unit, that is where I was first sent up. All of the cottages at Echo Glen had the exact schemas: four pods each with five rooms. Remember, tiers have bars and pods have doors. We went from panopticons to closed-caption surveillance. Toutle had extra security features such as solid wire mesh in between thick plastic windows. The rooms were bereft of any objects that could be used as projectiles or weapons (chairs, shelves, footlockers, etc.). At Toutle, I was introduced to bougie architectural elements, such as a foyer and a mudroom, that were foreign to my working poor background. Chores were now "details" and were rotated on a weekly basis. The lavatory was now called the nautical "head" probably because many of the staff were former members of the department of the navy. As the rooms did not have any plumbing or running water, when nature called you had to make a "head call." That is, request permission to use the head—that language is still in my damn repertoire—by summoning the staff with a pound on your door as piss bottles are major no-nos in lockdown units.

Toutle's foyer had two locked entrances where my shackles were removed before I was taken to the cottage's isolation room where I was strip-searched and had my contraband confiscated (a crudely sharpened state-issued toothbrush for morale and a Sharpie marker for tagging). The common area, a large square of roughly twenty-five seats, was empty save for two other occupants waiting to get processed out of lock-down: Baby Inch, a damu from Seattle who was photographed as a preteen in a National Geographic feature on Seattle's embattled Pike Street, and R—, an unaffiliated Chicano who was my fourth-grade classmate. R— was a pigeon-toed thief who got sent up for joyriding. He would later become a member of my archenemies, but at that time we were on good terms. He also let me know that there would only be three Chicanos in the cottage after his departure: Migs, Abe (pseudonym), and your boy. I knew neither of the other two personally, but Migs, who was from my home county, already had an infamous reputation that preceded him. Migs and I were kindred spirits and would grow tight with each other, while callously ostracizing Abe. That's right, when the brave turn cruel, those who are not fierce tend to succumb to the zealousness of fatalistically hardened youth.

Migs, at that time, was a lone wolf who was severely cross-eyed. It was a violently delicate subject that resulted in many a skirmish. He was always impeccably groomed with a fierce and confident presence. He was two years older than your boy and quick witted to boot. I mean, the vato had beaucoup institutional memory and institutional literacy, which, as you know, are two invaluable assets in surmounting the politics and the banal mental cruelties of everyday institutional life. In a world where a perceived or actual slight, however petty, is a slippery slope for one's reputation, his strategic thinking allowed him to anticipate and overcome potential conflicts. (Now, if that ain't mind-leading, you tell me what the hell is.)

The first time we spoke I aggravated him as he was looking away from me and at the wall. I committed a gangster no-no in shifting my gaze away from his lazy eye. I was more uncomfortable with his condition than he, who had been dealing it with his whole young life. Years later, in another lockdown unit in another institution, I came across one of Sartre's philosophical texts and was inundated with laughter when I noted the striking similarity between the abstracted, cock-eyed gaze of the French thinker and pistol-toting Migs. He was technically my enemy by then, but I sent him some good energy para que se cuidara de la envidia y el mal de ojo. Anyway, it took me some time to look at him the way he preferred people to look at him while he was speaking: right in the middle of his Mexibrows.

Whereas I was preemptively placed in lockdown by the administration, Migs was in Toutle for escaping from Echo Glen. In truth, he sawed through no bars, he burrowed no tunnels, nor did he take any hostages. Instead, he shimmied out of a window and conducted a night march (with no Boy Scout training) through five miles of dense forest and natural wetlands (Echo Glen is a fenceless facility) to a nearby gas station where he sat on a gas-station curb until he found a ride from an unsuspecting civilian family heading in the direction of his hometown known as the Palm Springs of Washington.

When I arrived at Toutle he was on a twenty-three and one program for pummeling a beast (in size and attitude). The offending party was a hulking white dude named Merlin, who had made the mistake of slighting him with an ethnic slur. Merlin was still puffed up in the face when I arrived at Toutle. Merlin may not have become enlightened by that skirmish, but he most certainly learned not to publicly crack Mexican jokes. It is unfortunate that violence oftentimes teaches one the value of common courtesy. This is one of the values of violence as practiced by bonded males: you will be held physically accountable for your words and actions. Free speech is a sacred concept, but hate speech is certainly not protected in those environments. Although Merlin certainly didn't disavow bigotry, he most certainly gained a better appreciation for the credible threat of violence courtesy of a cock-eyed Mexican.

One of my horrors was that I was more than the crime that I was sent up for. In fact, it was a crime that I did not even commit, but in my eagerness to experience incarceration, and to take the heat off of some older homies who actually committed the assault, I took full responsibility for the offense. And, kindly note that your boy doesn't do peer pressure. As a person of violence, I was unafraid of institutionalization and thrived in those settings. I was good with violence and doing time and I will always have to reckon with that. Oh, how I wish that I could forget that part of myself. I have no regrets—only some laments and one of those is that I had zealously committed myself to the tragic arts of violence in all four quadrants: physical, emotional, mental, and spiritual violence.

If we know anything about mass incarceration, it is that within and across that sinister coupling there is more punishment than crime. Even more troubling, we are all complicit in that sinister coupling where retribution prevails over account-ability. Therefore, it is the responsibility of each individual to enunciate our repudiation of our impardonable silence, and to discredit, delegitimize, and dismantle mass incarceration. If they could do it with the Gulag Archipelago of the former Soviet Union, then we can do it in the United States. It is a moral, ethical, and social imperative.

As an ex-con and a reformed gangster—both titles require a detached ruthlessness—I was among the most complex and worse. Incarceration did not dehumanize me—it was an element in which I thrived. My ethnic group, Chicanos and Latinos, are divided into two warring factions and we are structured, organized, and paramilitarized in our intergener-ational carceral experiences. Each time that I arrived at a new institution, I was attuned to the hierarchy and was cognizant of my contribution to obtaining, maintaining, and expanding my status and positioning. This hierarchy supersedes the indi-vidual and it is an unforgiving, meritocratic ecology that one is obliged to adapt to. This was an inheritance bestowed upon me by my elders, who in the mid-twentieth century began to self-organize their violent criminality behind the walls of gladiator schools. They were young gangsters who had a convict mindset. They were the true believers of the criminal underworld whose code was predicated on the credible threat of baroque displays of violence. That was the legacy that I inherited that allowed me to thrive in carceral institutions. So, you see, not all prisoners are convicts and it is the convicts who influence the everyday practices of the warehoused. For those who are not convicts, they serve two sentences. The first is meted out by the court, and the second is determined by the political influencers among the convicts. The prosecutors and the courts can say that they do not believe that prisons should be divided into predators and prey, but the prison ecosystem and male human nature prove otherwise. And, as a society, we are all complicit in that brutalizing dynamic as well.

It was many years after my release before I was holistically prepared to acknowledge how terrifying and dehumanizing incarceration could be for the multitudes who were overpunished in that sinister coupling. Within and across mass incarceration, the inmates are preyed upon by the convicts. The prison authorities mix the lambs with the wolves. In my experience, there is no such thing as treatment and rehabilitation in carceral institutions. If one wants to genuinely change, it is a grueling and desolate process of self-rehabilitation. And, prison authorities ought not to be allowed to say that there is treatment and rehabilitation in prisons. The prisoners, their families, and their communities as well as advocates in civil society ought to determine when one has been adequately held accountable and when one has changed. Social scientists may use the disease metaphor—how do we know when someone is cured?—but this pathological interrogative fails to determine how one has holistically transformed oneself. Yes, the few prisoners who have been reformed, changed, and transformed have largely done so through self-rehabilitation. That is one of the few genuine examples of transformation that I know of within and across the sinister coupling of mass incarceration.

A brutal fact about prisons is that once one is processed into one, it's not a Shakespearean question of what one would like to be, but what one has to become. This is when the brave can become cruel by preying on the weak. In Kenneth Hartman's riveting memoir, *Mother California*, he writes about being state-raised in California gladiator schools and jailhouses from the 1970s through the 2010s, and how he eventually refused to abjure his personal autonomy to the prison politics of his ethnicity.[1]

Male prisons, especially in the U.S. West and Southwest, are governed by fierce, self-segregating politics. It is an unforgiving hierarchy designed and implemented by the convicts. The two Mexican factions with their structures, the white convicts with their structure, the black convicts with their disorganized factions, and the "others" who must claim a respected space of their own on the yard and in the facility. Those who fall out of favor in these mainline politics are physically disciplined—ranging from a severe beating to a stabbing—and ostracized by the convicts and placed in Special Need Yards (protective custody) by prison authorities. Prisoners in protective custody are deemed "no good" and will perpetually be seen as undesirables by the convicts. The true believers are arbitrarily segregated by the administration in Intensive Management Units (the hole) and in Security Housing Units (the back, in the hole of the hole).

In *Mother California*, Hartman comes up with an alternative to Special Need Yards, called Honor Yards, which I think might offer a pathway to self-rehabilitation for many who are otherwise consigned to a purely punitive existence. He writes, "We need a name that reflects what is possible, that speaks to a higher purpose and provides the aspirational element we all hope for as a way out of the downward spiral. I settle on the Honor Yard Program, which reaches back into the history of California prisons and asks for something more out of the men."[2] In my view, Honor Yards might provide the genuine rehabilitation necessary for an atmosphere of accountability, healing, and transformation, whereas retributive warehousing perpetuates the dismal cycle of violence and recidivism.

As an autodidact who was self-taught and cell-taught, I did not have the opportunity to participate in an Honor Yard Program. As a zealous and militant believer in the underworld, I probably would not have deigned to participate in it as would most active members in prison politics. However, it is of paramount importance that an Honor Yard be an option for anyone who wants to *volunteer* to participate in that life-changing program with their name and dignity intact. Without it, the only other options for the true believers are the politics of the mainline and administrative segregation.

Allow me to provide two personal examples. First, I will center the concerns of a younger homie who I never did time with, but who confided in me his pride in my change and his own weariness with transformation. Writing from a closed custody yard, he cogently articulated his concerns. We'll call him D. In winter 2015, D wrote: "The trip is your transformation . . . I mean I'm happy to know that you've changed for the better & you've accomplished what you put your mind to but as a Gangster, a homie that I'm sure was hella down and committed, how did you just get up & change your life & leave what you [were] at one time ready to ride or die for? What was your thought process in those days? I would like to know cause I want to change for the better too but my thing is I can't leave this life in a dishonorable way such as a coward or ranker [defector], you know?" And, D continues: "I think

I could only change if the Barrio gave me their blessings & honored my decision." These were his ethical, legitimate concerns as a member in good-standing in the underworld. D's candor is dangerously admirable: "I've done half of my life locked up, I'm getting tired, I've had a lot of time to think & realize my mistakes and errors in life . . . I've just realized my sacrifices [were] in vain . . . this gangster life just don't make [sense] . . . at the same time it's sacred cause we just give so much to keep it alive. It almost feels like we've given [too] much & and have come [too] far to go back now . . . we're fighting a losing battle & our compass is broken."

As a reformed gangster who was once very active, my first thought was that his beliefs are weakening and that is a cardinal sin in the underworld. That is, to lose heart. But, D pivots: "Anyways, I'm getting off track, I do want change though homie. But I don't only want it for myself. I want it for the Barrio, this life ain't rite [sic]. We need to evolve & become a more positive, constructive & productive force." Wrapping it up, D says: "But yeah, that's a topic to be discussed at a later time. I just want to know your story threw [sic] your own words & I want to know what your thoughts are on 'change.' "

At the time, D was a respected member in the underworld hierarchy and within two years, he would place himself in a precarious situation that resulted in his ostracization from the underworld. His criminal virtue—to use Machiavelli's concept of a good prince—is now ruined. His worst dream, ostracization, became a reality and that is a very difficult wound to heal because it is an invisible wound. I advised him to focus on his personal transformation and not to disrupt or alienate the hierarchy of "the life" as that is a very different dynamic that would not be tolerated by the true believers. Respected members who have paid their dues can change, and the true believers will honor their change as long as they forever-live that change. That's an unwritten rule that is usually honored. One has to forever-more embody and exude that change. Civilians, I'll remind you that bonded males are anchored in selfless sacrifice and service to their street and institutional commitments.

Second, an alleged mobster and one of my revered elders in the feds, mi estimado Gato (RIP), wrote to me back in winter 2019—before he was beaten to death by a cowardly youngster in their SHU cell—and asked me a question that benignly shook me to my core. He was in his late seventies and had been consistently active in the life since the late 1950s. He was one of the most devoted fathers that I have ever known and as one of his brothers once told me: you know that someone is not a scumbag when their family still loves and communicates with them. Gato (RIP) wanted to know how I managed to create a cop-free living for myself after my last release when the nihilists among us would say that I had at least another bid, or two, in me.

Now, I have been asked many times about my change, but never from a person of that caliber, nor in the manner in which he asked it. My beloved late elder wanted to know how I changed with my name and dignity intact. Yowza. The words name and dignity spoke to me. My name was my reputation as both an active and inactive bonded male. I asked my elder to let me give that some more thought. Here's what I told the dear old man: each book, and there were thousands, in each cell, and there were tens of dozens in different institutions, gave me alternative and dignified ways of being without having to denounce nor debrief (snitch) against my brothers-in-arms. Now, I know that the flag-wavers, be they biased cops, retributive prosecutors, or pogue civilians, do not like to hear that, but kindly note that I have never sought their approval. God bless their hearts, especially after they left me hanging on the cross for close to nine years when I was a gung-ho man-child. Needless to say, I no longer live a life of violent criminality, nor do I endorse it. But, being self-taught and cell-taught catalyzed my transformation. Trust that dignified change can and ought to be by design. For the incarcerated that can be in an Honor Yard.

An honor yard, or pod, has to be a culture of shared accountability, rather than a slew of box-checking programs bereft of transformative substance and meaning. These are courageous spaces were prisoners are not expected to denounce or debrief the ecology of general population prison yards, whose ferocity varies from state to state. This is what is known as prison politics where the major ethnicities (Latino, white, and black) self-segregate into separate underworld hierarchies that vie for status and position. Prisoners who are ostracized from these politics are placed in Special Need Yards (also known as protective custody), which are despised by mainline prisoners as these yards house child molesters, rapists, informants, and former law enforcement officials. Many correctional officers also despise the prisoners housed in these yards.

As such, administrators and correctional officers ought to be highly experienced and embrace the localized tenets of the respective honor yard over arbitrary torments and punishment. In other words, prisoners as well as security and staff need to be highly vetted volunteers who develop a rapport anchored in accountability, transformation, and a dignified transition into civil society.

Most correctional facilities have at least one pod, where prisoners can immerse themselves in life-changing programs including educational (post-secondary opportunities), physical (yoga, stretching, and breath work), and immersive mental health practices that acknowledge the pain and trauma of their victims as well as their own.

These services can be provided by and funded from existing state funds, strategic philanthropic support, collegiate institutions invested in prisoner education, established non-profit organizations committed to dismantling mass incarceration, and volunteers who can share their professional and personal experiences with overcoming adversity and cultivating holistic practices of change. With increasing bipartisan support for criminal justice reform along with civil society's commitment to diminishing mass incarceration, honor yards are viable alternatives to warehousing prisoners, which cause and exacerbate pain. Honor yards, in contrast, hold prisoners morally responsible for their crimes, while not neglecting the possibilities of healing. They are places where people can change for the better and yet retain their inner, dignified selves.

Of course, these potential Honor Yards ought to be designed and implemented by prisoners themselves, their community members, concerned and contributing citizens, and, hopefully, with the input and contribution of survivors. As a doctor of letters who is still ruthlessly pragmatic, I'll submit that a proactive component of any potential Honor Yard ought to have a nexus of literature, art, and justice. The arts—literature, poetry, testimonios, music, painting, and craftwork—were crucial in my transformation. And justice in its truest sense is anchored in actualized accountability, healing for both the survivor who inflicted the pain and the survivor who strives to surmount that pain, thorough transformation, and a restorative transition into civil society.

Also, each Honor Yard has to have a stellar educational component such as Bard's Prison Initiative.[3] Civil society, from the individual do-gooder to the nonprofit organization, ought to provide genuinely transformative services that range from breath work and meditation, to yoga and underwater basket weaving. And, logistically, every Honor Yard ought to have prison administrators and correctional officers who sincerely embrace the central tenets of that Honor Yard. In other words, the prisoners as well as the prison officials need to be highly vetted volunteers committed to transformation. As each state differs in its respective prison ecology, I will refrain from being too specific, while emphasizing these macro solutions. The micro solutions ought to begin with prisoner input because it is they who truly know the ecology (the existential dynamics) of their respective prisons.

And there needs to be an enduring rapport among all of those involved in the sustainability of an Honor Yard. That is, with people who have justice in their hearts. Just people who have a passionate belief in discovering the beauty and the best in the punished. Just people who have a sense of human kinship. Just people who are also committed to the aftercare of prisoners beyond their release. Just people who want to awaken the conscience of how their society treats and cares for the imprisoned. Just people committed to human fairness. A just society that refuses to make profits out of punishing prisoners. A just society that rejects the retributive principle on a mass scale for healing.

8

Undebatable

Daniel S. Throop

Daniel Throop was president of the Norfolk Prison Debating Society and has written for VICE. Born in Meadville, Pennsylvania, he is currently incarcerated in Massachusetts for charges of aggravated rape, robbery, and attempted murder stemming from a 2004 home invasion. He holds a BA in Interdisciplinary Studies from Boston University and a paralegal certificate from Blackstone Career Institute, and is a longtime member of Toastmasters International and the Partakers College Behind Bars program. Throop is an accomplished public speaker who enjoys using his voice to advocate for meaningful social justice reforms with a particular focus on educational equality. He proposes the creation of a National Prison Debate League.

"The only way to modify the behavior of prisoners is to put their heads on the curb and stomp them," recently quipped a Massachusetts Department of Correction officer to three of his black-shirted brothers within my hearing. Sycophantic laughter was their response, and remarkably, I overheard this exchange while drafting this very essay on prison reform. The false bravado of these men aside, I have to acknowledge that the officer who made this crude remark is right about one thing: targeting our prisoners' heads is the answer. We simply differ on tactics.

For far too long, the politics of punishment has been informed by those who endorse head-busting attitudes. Of the six hundred thousand prisoners released every year in the U.S., 70 percent of them are re-arrested within five years.[1] Clearly, everyone is losing under the status quo. And yet education, the most powerfully transformative tool in the rehabilitative arsenal, remains largely unsupported by policy makers. A 2014 RAND Corporation study found that participation in correctional education reduces recidivism by 43 percent, on average.[2] I have a plan to do much better than that 43 percent reduction rate, along with a proof of concept that's undebatable.

Since most prisoners have never attended college, I propose bringing colleges to prisons through academic debates. The introduction of college students into the prison environment offers a unique opportunity for social diplomacy and collaboration. For those incarcerated, these interpersonal connections can be profoundly aspirational, and for the students these experiences are revelatory in their erasure of negative prison stereotypes. As someone who has successfully organized five separate debate events against three different colleges, at two different Massachusetts prisons, I know that this formula works. My plan is to expand this model through the creation of a National Prison Debate League, with member teams from every state and federal institution throughout the United States.

While the vast majority of U.S. prisons do not offer any college programming, they do possess the basic components required for a "build it and they will come" approach.[3] The raw human talent is ever-present, and with a uniform training curriculum to help teams get started across facilities, a strong foundation can be established nationwide and cost-free. No special infrastructure is necessary, as every prison has a classroom or library in which teams can meet, strategize, and conduct research as they prepare arguments and organize events. Tier and yard times can also be utilized for planning and practicing purposes.*

The debate league should be founded as a nonprofit organization governed by an external board of directors who can raise funds, develop teams, provide resources, and operate a website that highlights the work of its members, all in an effort to re-humanize our prisoner population for those outside the system. By shining a much-needed light on our many unheralded success stories, the league would also provide a direct rebuttal to the negative portrayals of prisoners that dominate news outlets and cloud public perceptions of us. Perhaps, as a performance measure, we can even track the recidivism data of our members in comparison with the national average.

Prison teams, once formed, can establish a season schedule corresponding with the spring and fall semesters of their local

---

* "Tier time" and "yard time" refer to blocks of free time in a prison's common areas or outdoors.

colleges and host debates within their respective prisons. Institutional program staff can facilitate all the requisite clearances for these debates, just as they do for all other volunteers and guests who enter prisons routinely for special events. Travel costs and security concerns would probably prove prohibitive when it comes to inter-prison team debates, but the collegiate contests would accomplish more than enough, especially in creating an interface through which these experiences positively shape the attitudes and opinions of our future leaders and policy makers about incarcerated people. Every event would be an opportunity to showcase the tremendous human potential and intellectual capacity of our incarcerated population, while also nudging our schools to invest their educational resources in the American prison system.

The Boston University Prison Education Program (BU-PEP) was founded through a very similar process, thanks to the historic accomplishments of the Norfolk Prison Debating Society. The Norfolk society was one of the greatest debate teams and prison success stories of all time. Between 1933 and 1966, Norfolk proved its worth by destroying the best college teams in the Northeast, with a record of 144 wins and 8 losses.[4] Malcolm X himself was a member, and it was during his time with the team that he developed his famously fiery public speaking skills. Professor Elizabeth "Ma" Barker took notice of the Norfolk society and convinced Boston University president John Silber to implement the BU program in 1972.[5]

The moral courage that BU leadership has displayed in stepping up to support prison education, especially after Pell Grants were eliminated for prisoners in 1994, has been nothing short of inspirational.[6] The fact that BU program graduates have a less than one percent recidivism rate speaks for itself in proving my case.[7] Prison debate brings colleges behind our walls, and college degrees drastically improve outcomes for the justice-involved and stop the revolving prison door. The only question left to answer is: Why aren't states funding such postsecondary correctional education programs, when their effectiveness is indisputable?

In terms of "getting what you pay for," prison policy makers appear to be running a rehabilitative-service Ponzi scheme on American taxpayers. In 2013, eleven states spent more on corrections than on higher education, and in 2016, the United States spent over $80 billion on incarceration.[8] Despite having massive correctional budgets, states are failing to make any real investments in postsecondary correctional education programs for their incarcerated populations, which are made up of socially disadvantaged men and women who need education to transcend the negative cycle of release and incarceration.

Massachusetts is a perfect example of this prison Ponzi scheme. On its surface, the state is widely regarded as a great bastion of both liberalism and higher learning. Indeed, it is home to some of the best schools in the world, and both of its U.S. senators are blue enough to make Sinatra's optometrist proud. However, a closer look reveals that the state's executive branch oversees a Department of Correction that seems to reflect different sentiments about rehabilitation. The DOC's mission statement reads, "Promote public safety by managing offenders while providing care and appropriate programming in preparation for successful reentry into the community."[9] But the DOC's budget tells a different story.

According to a 2014 report on the DOC's budget, that year inmate programs accounted for only 1.98 percent of the total DOC operating budget of $562 million.[10] Of 5,177 full-time employees in 2015, only 83, or a mere 1.6 percent, were educational staff.[11] Even the most ardent supporters of law enforcement and tough criminal justice policies must acknowledge that their tax dollars are being used counterproductively here, as most prisoners in Massachusetts will be returning to their communities with no employable new skills because corrections officials prefer to employ a maintenance staff over an educational one by a greater than two-to-one margin—180 to 83, respectively.[12] Again, we're getting what we pay for.

It's important to note that the BU program receives zero funding from the state, but offers free scholarships for corrections staff. James Matesanz, a former superintendent and current director of the Boston program, writes in *Corrections Today*: "In addition to supplementing BU-PEP programming, Boston University provides a significant number of scholarships to Massachusetts Department of Correction (MADOC) staff who wish to pursue further education. Several past and current leaders in the MADOC have benefited, and continue to benefit, from the staff scholarship program. This mitigates some of the potential resentment about the program in the institutions."[13]

All scholarships for prisoners were canceled for the 2017–2018 academic year, but staff scholarships continued unabated.[14] In light of Matesanz's extensive background with the MADOC, such a diversion of PEP resources appears to represent an unethical conflict of interest. When my Norfolk Inmate Council's Education Committee colleagues and

I dared to question this decision, we were accused of being ungrateful and were warned that voicing our concerns would get the program shut down. Instilling fear is the MADOC's go-to move whenever its control is questioned, but what it fears most is losing control of public perception. The time has come for the public to understand that not all the bad guys in the system are the ones wearing stripes.

As for my own stripes, I have worked diligently to transform myself through educational pursuits over fifteen years and counting of incarceration. My proposals for positive change are directly drawn from experience. When I entered the system back in 2004, I was a twenty-five-year-old "out-of-state fugitive," as the district attorney put it. He wasn't wrong. I left Pennsylvania to avoid arrest for local probation warrants and came to Massachusetts to lay low for a while until I could figure out my next move. I never got that far, though, because after one very drunken and drug-fueled night of partying, I woke up in a holding cell charged with rape, robbery, and attempted murder. Horrified, I took full responsibility for my actions, and the court gave me an eighteen- to twenty-two-year prison sentence. Ashamed, abandoned, and utterly alone, I walked into a prison system where I knew no one—not even myself.

Once the shell shock of my new reality began to dissipate, I set about the task of self-improvement. Disgusted with myself and the destructive nature of my former lifestyle, I committed my full energies to change and haven't wavered since. Introspection, education, and communication became the primary tools of my reconstruction. Perhaps most importantly, I finally learned how to get out of my own way so that

I could begin to move forward. Once I picked myself up, I became active in program leadership and used my abilities to pick up others. It felt good. Instead of confirming other people's stereotypes of prisoners by fighting against my new peers, I fought with and for them to improve our collective condition and mutual quality of life.

Combining my communication skills with my passion for learning led me to form my first prison debate team in 2006, while I was at Old Colony Correctional Center. Debate teaches critical thinking and conflict resolution skills, and in lieu of formal college classes, it provided us a desperately needed source of education. On June 16, 2009, my work garnered me an opportunity to meet with then governor of Massachusetts Deval Patrick and his staff to discuss prison programs and educational needs. I told Governor Patrick that I saw debate as a "vehicle for intellectual equality," and he acknowledged my vision as "having merit." Not only was I honored to have such an opportunity, but this also proved to be a watershed moment for me: I realized that using my voice to advocate for policy reforms is what I wanted to do.

At Old Colony, we hosted debates against Bridgewater State University (formerly Bridgewater State College) three times from 2009 to 2010. My teammates and I went on to win all three contests. I transferred to MCI-Norfolk in 2010 to seek entry into the BU program and was accepted in 2011. In 2014, I co-authored a book about prison reform with my friend James Keown and a group of Harvard students entitled *Corrective Lenses*.[15] I'd also brought my debate training model from Old Colony Correctional Center with me to Norfolk, and after assembling a strong new team and finally convincing prison officials to give us a chance to revive the legendary Norfolk Prison Debating Society, I was able to set up an event with Boston College's prestigious Fulton Debating Society in 2016.

Drawn to the rich history of the Norfolk society, journalist Natasha Haverty covered the Boston College debate for NPR and broadcast our winning efforts to the world.[16] With our abilities no longer a secret, we were able to book MIT in 2017. I also completed my bachelor's degree from Boston University and proudly graduated magna cum laude earlier that same year. Sadly, the MIT debate would turn out to be my last. Barely a week later, I was abruptly transferred from Norfolk to the Massachusetts Treatment Center, which is basically the Massachusetts system's version of Siberia.

I suspect that my banishment was retaliatory in nature, but I suppose that is the price to be paid for opening so many doors in a place known for keeping them locked. I have no regrets about that at all. In fact, I am proud of the ambassadorial role that I've been able to play in honorably representing both myself and the human community of prisoners that society at large has too quickly discarded. Since my departure, I've done my best to promote the Norfolk society from afar while James Keown keeps the team moving in the right direction.

The prison debate model works, and the world has been taking notice. Norfolk engaged Harvard in 2018 and Cornell and Boston College in 2019. Our success has been reported on by NPR, the *Marshall Project*, and the *New Yorker*, and has also generated interest in turning our story into both a book and a movie.[17] With every event, more eyes are being opened as we continue to remind society of our human value and redemptive potential. But Massachusetts represents only one-fiftieth of the national equation. Imagine if our efforts were to be replicated across the country.

A national prisoners' debate league is a solution to the problem of educational inequality in U.S. prisons. If we had the opportunity to meet collegiate debaters, the country's future leaders and policy makers, and show them our true capabilities through head-to-head debates, we would have a profound impact on the prevailing attitudes toward incarcerated people. Perhaps this would allow the politics of punishment to be softened, paving the way for the funding of more postsecondary correctional educational programs.

9

A Call for Pardons

Khalil A. Cumberbatch

Khalil A. Cumberbatch is a nationally recognized formerly incarcerated advocate working at the intersection of criminal justice and immigration policy change. He has worked with the reentry community in New York since 2010, when he was released after serving almost seven years in New York State prisons. Since his release, Cumberbatch has worked with various nonprofits as a service provider, policy analyst, advisor, board member, collaborator, and consultant. He currently serves as chief strategist at New Yorkers United for Justice. He proposed expanded use of executive pardons.

On a spring day like any other, I woke up in my apartment in Queens and went about my daily ritual of making coffee and watching the morning news. Next on my schedule was waking up my daughters and getting them ready for school. The sun was shining, and so was my spirit, because I was just one week away from completing my master's degree in social work. Ever since I had been released from incarceration,

I meticulously planned every step toward obtaining my degree, including working at various nonprofits, as both an intern and an employee, in addition to my schoolwork.

I was so close, I could taste it. This would be the fulfillment of a promise I had made to my wife and myself about changing my legacy to reflect who I really was: a person who, despite having been incarcerated, had potential. But when my doorbell rang at 7 a.m., agents from Immigration and Customs Enforcement were waiting outside. "Good morning," one officer said to me. "We're conducting an investigation and would like to come in, to ask you a few questions." "Couldn't I answer the questions here?" I asked, standing in my doorway. "It would be easier if we asked you privately," the officer responded.

The agents resembled the NYPD in their dress and demeanor, armed and wearing bullet-proof vests. I didn't have anything to hide, so I let them in. Once they entered my living room, where my wife and I sat on the couch, the men told me the real reason for their visit. They were going to arrest me based on my criminal conviction from over a decade ago: a robbery I committed as a twenty-year-old, for which I had already served time. Coupled with the fact that I was a legal permanent resident—I'm from Guyana originally, but I have lived in Queens with my family since I was a toddler—my record made me eligible for detention and deportation proceedings. My heart stopped. The terror and fear that overcame me were deafening. I was unable to comprehend what they were saying. I could only see their mouths moving. I felt sick to my stomach and couldn't stand. I eventually composed myself enough to hear them say that I was going to be presented to an immigration judge, who would make a decision on my case. The only thing I could say in response was, "How long is this going to take? I have class tonight." They told me I'd be home by the end of the day.

By that night, I was at a jail in Kearny, New Jersey, all alone in a double-bunk cell with no idea of what was going to happen next. Jail cells have a distinct smell: bleach and concrete, mixed with dirty mop head. The odor brought me right back to the maximum-security prison where I had originally served my sentence. I couldn't stop thinking of my daughters. They had never been separated from me, and I couldn't imagine what they were going through. I thought of my wife, too. That morning, she had woken up in a two-parent household, but by now she had gone to sleep as the single caretaker of two little girls. I had promised never to leave her and my daughters, yet here I was, breaking that vow—all because of a bad decision I had made at a very distant and different time in my life.

Instead of being back at home within a day, that night was the first of a five-month odyssey through the immigration detention system. The intake housing unit I was placed in was bitter cold; lo and behold, they called it "the freezer." Even though it was May, people wore long johns and were covered in blankets because the air-conditioning was kept at such chilling temperatures.[1] The food was horrible. There is not a jail or prison in the country where food is "good," but my first meal back in detention after being outside for four years absolutely disgusted me. Technically, it was "oatmeal." If you've ever had bad, re-microwaved oatmeal, multiply that yuck by one thousand, and you still can't fully understand how gross this was.

Breakfast was served at 5:30 a.m., and all I could think was, yesterday, at this time, I was in my own house, with my family, sleeping. I'm naturally drawn to people. I want to learn about them, about their history, their culture, their stories, their struggles. But in jail, you can't allow yourself to be open. It was hard enough for me to accept that I was not just incarcerated, but re-incarcerated. I couldn't bring myself to embrace the experience by telling the other people there that I wanted to learn about them. I remember my phone calls with my daughters. My youngest was no more than three years old at the time, and whenever she would get on the phone with me, she would ask, "Daddy, when are you coming home?" My wife had done the most humane thing she believed she could do, which was to tell them that I'd gone on a business trip. In a child's mind, if you choose to leave home, you can also choose to return. Thus, my youngest daughter wanted to know when I was going to choose to return home. I didn't know what the outcome of my detention was going to be; all I knew was that there was a high likelihood that I would not be able to go home to my daughter, and that what she was suffering through now, at three years old, was going to become her entire life. But then, after many months, and with little explanation, I was released.

The day I left immigration detention, I remember being awakened early in the morning and getting told simply to pack all of my stuff. The officer didn't know where I was going. It was 3:30 a.m. By 6 a.m., after a bus ride, I was in the courthouse. By 11 a.m., I was released into the custody of my family. The first person who greeted me was my older daughter, who ran to me with tears in her eyes and hugged me as hard as a seven-year-old can squeeze anyone. I told her that I was sorry—sorry that I had left her, sorry that I had caused her so much pain. She looked me in the eyes and said, "Daddy, that's okay. I always knew you'd be coming home." When I think back on my time in immigration detention, I think of how much heartache incarcerating someone temporarily but indefinitely, and doing so while sharing barely any information, can cause them and their family. I was very fortunate to have a tremendous amount of legal and community support that ultimately gave me the opportunity to be released. In December 2014, New York governor Andrew Cuomo granted me an executive pardon to prevent my deportation, which is exceedingly rare in these kinds of cases.[2] However, I am devastated by the fact that there were other people out there, both in detention and already deported, people just like me—and just like you—who won't get the same outcome.

During the past seven years, the United States has deported over two million people, with approximately 880,000 of them targeted because of a prior criminal conviction.[3] Additionally, the U.S. has deported more people in the last ten years than in the previous one hundred.[4] Bolstered by decades of "tough on crime" rhetoric and, most recently, by the so-called war on terror, the deportation apparatus has ballooned. The budget for the Department of Homeland Security, which houses Immigration and Customs Enforcement, has grown from $9 billion in 1995 to $19.5 billion in 2000 to over $56 billion in 2011.[5] The Illegal Immigration Reform and Immigrant Responsibility Act (IIRIRA) of 1996 vastly expanded the criminal offenses (otherwise referred to as aggravated felonies) that make a person deportable and also severely restricted the ability of a judge to waive a person's potential deportation.[6]

Recently, much attention has been given to potential solutions to mass incarceration—from expanding community corrections to reclassifying certain felony offenses as misdemeanors. In similar fashion, the use of executive clemency power has been utilized by state governors and even by President Obama. However, it is important to note that clemency power is carried out in two distinct ways—commutations and pardons—and a commutation only amounts to changing a punishment to one that is less severe. For a person who is a non-citizen, the use of commutation power is merely an exercise of power to significantly reduce their prison sentence, which in many cases results in almost immediate release. However, commutations do nothing to relieve the collateral consequences of a criminal conviction, including immigration consequences.

The second use of power that falls under clemency is the pardon. Under the U.S. Constitution, the executive branch, which includes the president and state governors, is given the power to "grant reprieves and pardons for offenses against the United States, except in cases of impeachment." Pardons, unlike commutations, eliminate the discriminatory collateral consequences of a criminal conviction. Regarding immigration policy, granting a pardon almost exclusively eliminates immigration consequences that put non-citizens at risk for deportation.

In the effort to reduce mass incarceration and find alternative ways to hold individuals accountable with a reasonable form of punishment, there needs to be a greater level of consciousness for people who are non-citizens, as they do not receive the full benefit of many criminal justice reforms that are being proposed. This was demonstrated, for example, in the federal Department of Justice's decision in October 2015 to release approximately six thousand men and women from federal prison. Of the six thousand people who were released, approximately fourteen hundred were non-citizens who, once released from the federal prison system, were then funneled into the immigration detention system, where they could languish for an additional six to twelve months, at an additional cost to taxpayers, with almost inevitable deportation.[7] The use of clemency power in the form of pardons would have eliminated the immigration consequences from those convictions, allowing those fourteen hundred people to be released to their families and communities.

Current federal immigration policies dictate that anyone who is a non-citizen and who is convicted of a criminal offense is eligible to have deportation proceedings initiated. Furthermore, anyone convicted of an "aggravated felony"—a classification for a list of specific charges, some of which are neither aggravated nor felonies—is subject to mandatory detention and almost inevitable deportation. Therefore, non-citizens with criminal convictions are subjected to an extreme level of punishment that extends from that criminal conviction, irrespective of how much prison time they already served, their length of stay in the United States before the conviction, their community and family ties, their record of healthy societal engagement, or any other possible reason against deportation.

I propose the expanded use of pardon power to alleviate the added consequences of a criminal conviction for non-citizens. In this way, one of the most severe collateral punishments for having a criminal conviction will be significantly reduced. Such steps have already been taken by certain states, including Georgia and New York.[8] The state of Georgia's Board of Pardons set up a special panel to review pardon applications for people facing deportation on the basis of a retroactive application of the IIRIRA. Close to 140 immigration pardons were granted during the period of review from 2000 to 2001. In New York State, then governor David Paterson also created a special panel to review pardon applications that would relieve immigration consequences. In 2010, Governor Paterson granted six of those applications.[9]

The recent public attention to mass incarceration is encouraging. States are taking progressive steps to address the sheer number of people who are ensnared in the web of the criminal justice system, including employing the use of the executive branch's clemency powers. While many criminal justice advocates have pushed for the commutation of prison sentences, primarily for people with nonviolent drug offenses, there is very little energy among advocates or philanthropic resources for using existing measures that would significantly reduce the immigration consequences for non-citizens with criminal convictions. The movement for reform must be more responsive to and inclusive of immigrants by turning their efforts toward pardons instead of commutation alone. Every governor in this country has been entrusted to use pardon power to right some of the wrongs doled out by the criminal justice system. For non-citizens, those wrongs can include literal banishment via deportation. Governors and even the president have the ability to reunite families and stop excessive punishments that far supersede the ones given by criminal courts. The time is now to use those powers more broadly.

10

Over-Incarceration and Gain Time: What's Wrong and How to Fix It

Jeremiah Paul Cahours

Jeremiah Cahours was born and raised in Michigan. After moving around a lot in his early twenties he finally settled in Panama City Beach, Florida, with his wife and daughter. Cahours is a devout Christian and is passionate about prison reform as a result of his firsthand exposure through incarceration since 2013. He calls for a shift in sentencing and the use of good-time credits.

I've been searching for justice inside this unjustifiable system since 2013. That year, my long-held belief in our government's commitment to justice—demonstrated through checks and balances, the inalienable right to due process, and other measures—was shattered. I saw our criminal justice system for what it is: a shaky façade covering the corruption of a long-broken system meant to line the pockets of politicians and break the backs, lives, and families of those subjected to its exploitation. It is a living beast that must be fed. It does not matter if you fancy yourself an upstanding, tax-paying citizen. Everyone has, at one point in time, done something that was technically unlawful.

I was raised with the belief that only "bad" people go to prison. If someone was behind bars, I assumed they "deserved" to be there. Now I've learned firsthand that such ideas are far from absolute. I've met men who served prison time for driving on a suspended license, contracting without a permit, and being addicted to opioids. I've seen men brought back on probation violations for reasons as trivial as being out five minutes past their curfew—because their wife was in the hospital—or for moving from their place of residence two days sooner than they were supposed to, even though they were forced to do so because their home was flooding. I know the system is broken. I am a witness of it every day, and am living it every moment.

This country, and especially Florida, has a heartbreaking track record of over-incarcerating. Studies show that the length of a potential prison sentence is not a deterrent for crime.[1] If you're going to do something illegal, knowledge of the length of your possible incarceration is likely the furthest thing from your mind. Therefore, mandatory minimum sentences and lengthy periods of incarceration do nothing but offer consolation to victims and their families, while simultaneously punishing the prisoner's family as well as society as a whole.

The cost of incarceration goes far beyond the initial price tag of daily expenses per inmate, billed to the law-abiding general populace. A well-documented study published by the Pew Research Center demonstrates the negative impact a felony record has on an individual's societal and economic future.[2] Everything, from the amount of money the individual can earn to how far they can advance in their career, is affected. This trickles down through a person's immediate family, to their children and grandchildren, creating a downward spiral of economic negativity. Are there incarcerated individuals who are able to move beyond and excel in spite of this? Yes, of course. But statistics demonstrate the rule, not the exception. I am not advocating lawlessness or anarchy, and I believe in immutable laws and the moral code of God and man: if you do wrong, you should be punished. At the same time, I believe it is unconscionable that someone who drives on a suspended license would receive prison time alongside much more violent criminals.

The prison industrial complex is vast, complicated, inhumane, and rife with conflicts of interest. An ex-governor of Florida, where I am incarcerated, is married to a woman on the board of the private health care company contracted to serve the inmates in the state's Department of Correction. Do you suppose the ex-governor might have a monetary interest in keeping the prison population high? As a firsthand witness, I can assure you that the adage "Once you're in the system, it's impossible to get out" is true.

Now why, do you suppose, would that be? Part of the issue lies with how ex-felons are perceived in society, and consequently treated because of it. How they are repeatedly punished for past sins. The other part is how the incarcerated are subjected to unfair practices in prison, which reinforce negative behavior and ultimately lead to recidivism. That is the part I would like to address.

Recidivism has long been a big issue for the prison system, and it warrants a critical investigation and a bold, unconventional initiative to solve it. Another famous saying goes, "An ounce of prevention is worth a pound of cure." As someone who was and still is generally a law-abiding individual, I'm honestly not quite sure how to prevent others from being "railroaded" into the system. But what I am qualified to do is take the same saying and apply it to recidivism. How can we do better to ensure that an individual will not recidivise? It starts with choices. If you don't teach an individual how to make good choices in prison, you cannot expect them to make good choices once they re-enter society.

The awarding of meritorious gain time—the awarding of an earlier release date for good behavior—is a program widely used by prisons as a failing attempt to produce the behavior that officials feel is conducive to a more positive environment as well as the safety of staff and prisoners. It works by gifting a set number of days per week or month to an inmate who has earned them through his or her conduct, appearance, hygiene, work attitude, or other positive behaviors.

Some states award gain time for the successful completion of programs involving things like GED testing, vocational instructions, life skills training, and drug prevention. In theory, this all sounds good—however, in practice it is more complicated.

The first issue with this particular method of behavior modification is the existence of mandatory minimum sentences. These sentences, which Florida has implemented with reckless abandon, do not allow anyone serving them from earning *any* gain time, period. If you are sentenced to seven years under a mandatory minimum guideline, you will spend exactly seven years, to the day, behind bars. In these instances, the reward-punishment system becomes moot. Mandatory minimums effectively take away the state's ability to attempt rehabilitation long before that individual even enters the system through incarceration.

If an individual knows that disobeying the rules will prevent them from earning gain time, that individual is more likely to do what is required. You cannot expect a person with a track record of poor decision making to automatically start making good choices simply because they are now in prison. From my fairly lengthy period of observation, I've learned that the majority of inmates will continue to do what they've always done until they get sick and tired, or until they are shown that good choices can lead to positive outcomes. And it is in these overly rigid sentences that the second and most problematic facet of the current gain-time program comes into play.

In Florida, according to the statutes governing the Department of Corrections, an individual sentenced to prison time must complete a minimum of 85 percent of the imposed sentence. Satisfactorily earned gain time is awarded at ten days per calendar month, along with a couple of additional instances in which you can earn extra gain time. However, if I am earning 120 gain-time days per calendar year, I should be knocking off about 33 percent of my imposed sentence, and should only have to serve around 67 percent of that time. But since I am required to do 85 percent, the math doesn't work. In essence, the state is allowed to steal gain time that I rightfully earned. Eighty-five percent of 365 days per year equals

310 days, which means that at the most, I can actually earn only a 55-day yearly reduction in my imposed sentence.

A good friend of mine gave me this great illustration of this arrangement that really hammers this point home: I am the owner of a Widget factory. You and I enter into an employment contract in which we agree that I will pay you $1,200 per pay period. As my employee, you do all that is asked and required of you during that pay period. Payday rolls around and you excitedly open your paycheck, only to discover that instead of the agreed upon $1,200, your check only contains $550. Outraged, you demand an explanation. "Oh," I say, "I held back the other $650 just in case you mess up in the future. You know, if you don't show up one day, or if maybe you break something. Basically, I'm keeping that for if you screw up."

By keeping, or stealing, sixty-five of my rightfully earned gain-time days per year, the state is actively rewarding and promoting negative behavior and punishing good behavior. On the surface this may not seem like a big deal, but there are several reasons why it is.

This hypocritical system of meritorious gain time fosters an atmosphere of lawlessness within the prison system. I personally know multiple men who have used the corruption of the gain-time system to their advantage. They spent much of their time in prison smuggling and selling tobacco, various drugs, cell phones, and even jewelry and watches, but because of the way gain time works, they were then able to make up "lost" time and *still* go home at their 85 percent date. Because prison is like high school on steroids, replete with gossip and rumormongering, everyone inside is aware of this. What kind of message does that send? Do the right thing and you'll go home at an 85 percent date—or illegally earn thousands of dollars (one man I know made $60,000 in about five months, and another one over a period of years bought a house and two cars for cash), and *still* go home at your 85 percent date. In prison, if you pay attention, you learn the best ways to work the system. Do you think that helps or hurts a person's moral compass and their effort to make good, positive choices?

Beyond setting the stage for high recidivism and causing the prison system to be rampant with illegal activity, this current gain-time farce has far-reaching negative effects in the local communities containing these facilities as well. The state's budget for its Department of Corrections was $2.4 billion in 2018, so for a population of approximately one hundred thousand inmates (it fluctuates either way by around six to nine thousand per year), taxpayers are covering a daily expense of sixty-three dollars per inmate.[3] Though this is one of the lowest budgets for state corrections in the country (which manifests in our subpar conditions and the bare minimum care required to squeak through the hoops of federal regulation), it is still unfair to the citizens of this state.

The state (that is, taxpayers) had to pay $1,916 per month of room and board for a fellow inmate of mine who was sentenced to two years in prison for driving on a suspended license (and from my personal knowledge, he's not the only one with that same story). Instead of having to do some community service and pay a fine, which is probably a lot closer to what his punishment should have been and which would have asked him to give *back* to the state, the state now has to pay for him.

If we break down these numbers, they reveal a fascinating—and infuriating—reality. If I and the rest of Florida's one hundred thousand inmates were each allowed to keep those sixty-five days per year that we rightfully earned through meritorious gain time, we would be going home sixty-five days per incarcerated year sooner. At sixty-three dollars per day, that's $4,095 per inmate that the state would be saving every year. If you take that yearly savings and apply it to the number of inmates in the state's penal system, the total comes to a whopping $409.5 million per year. Considering that dollar figure constitutes almost 18 percent of the state's annual corrections budget, I can think of a lot more programs that could use that money. Education, infrastructure, any number of underfunded social programs—the list is practically endless. Reforming meritorious gain-time policies would have nothing to do with being either "soft" or "hard" on crime. It would be about rewarding good behavior while simultaneously teaching inmates how to make good choices by giving them what they rightfully earn through those choices.

I have one final point of contention concerning how our current gain-time system is misleading and incorrect. Suppose that I was able to keep all of my earned gain time, meaning that if I were sentenced to ten years of prison, I could earn 1,200 days of gain time (ten days per month at 120 months). This would mean that I might only have to complete 66 percent of my sentence (before changes in 1995, the minimum was 65 percent of the imposed sentence). For each month that I earn gain time, my end-of-sentence date moves ten days closer, meaning I will go home before getting to apply my full 120 months of gain time to my sentence. Though this might sound good, there is a catch. If I were to do 66 percent of a 120-month sentence (ten years), in theory, I would go home after serving 79 months—roughly six and a half years. However, the current system operates like two trains traveling toward each other at different speeds: eventually they will meet, but not in the middle, because one train is traveling faster than the other. If Florida's legislature were to repeal the 86 percent mandate and bring back the 65 percent that it used to be, while keeping the same gain time accrual rate, one would still have to serve nearly 75 percent of their sentence. Even if accrual of gain time was changed from 10 days to 20 days per month, you still have the same issues with not getting to keep all of it as described earlier.[4] Rather than a complete overhaul of the system, I propose a few simple tweaks and changes centered on the idea that one thing incentivizes all prisoners, regardless of specific circumstances or backgrounds: going home earlier.

An individual sentenced to time in prison should be awarded all of their potential gain time up front, giving them the responsibility to keep it. I can't speak for the rest of the country, but in Florida, that would mean inmates could get a third of their sentences taken off right out of the gate. I understand why this might not sound fair to the average person. If you can do the crime, you can do the time, right? I can't tell you how many times I heard that platitude growing up, or how many times I repeated it myself. This change in gain-time policy would mark an extremely important, but subtle, shift in cultural attitudes toward the incarcerated. By offering inmates gain time up front and then holding them accountable for keeping it, the system would empower them to make the choices that will affect their entire future, starting with when they get to go home.

Every month, we prisoners are handed a gain-time sheet that shows us our current end-of-sentence date and how it has been affected by the gain time we earned for that particular period. If we could get our gain time up front, our gain-time sheets would become even more powerful visual tools. If an individual decided to act against the rules and regulations of the department, he or she would physically see and psychologically feel the results of those actions through their end-of-sentence date moving in the wrong direction. If somebody decides not to straighten up their bedding area, for instance, and their next gain-time sheet shows that their end-of-sentence date has moved back three days, they will likely be more willing to comply in the future. Unlike the current broken system, which allows for a wide highway of wiggle room for disobedience, under the new system the time this inmate loses from not making their bed will not be given back. Also, in the new system, certain stipulations for earning gain time can be made to help those inmates with a prior history of misconduct who have demonstrated positive shifts in attitude.

The positive consequences of this paradigm shift in the system could fundamentally change our culture's views about punishment. An individual who learns to make good choices that affect their future before they return to society will have a much higher probability of achieving success. Whether it's in their job, through their education, or with their family, society as a whole will be better off for it. When this individual gets to go home sixty-five days per year sooner, they will not only save the state unnecessary and wasteful expenditure, but will also pay the system back as a contributing member of society. We must not delay in taking a long necessary look at our failing prison system. Empowering our incarcerated population is one of our most powerful tools to unlock this country's latent potential. Rewarding good behavior is within our grasp, and it's time we began to do so.

11

From Coming Home to Running the Homecoming Project

Terah Lawyer

Terah Lawyer is a program manager for the Homecoming Project at Impact Justice in the San Francisco Bay Area. Her lived experience as a formerly incarcerated woman who spent fifteen years in prison informs her work and motivates her to inspire others in taking a proactive role in finding solutions to local problems. Lawyer has been an advocate for incarcerated people for more than a decade as a peer health educator, and a drug and alcohol counselor, while sitting on the boards of Justice Now and California Prison Focus. Lawyer proposes an innovative approach to leveraging the sharing economy to provide housing for people coming out of prison.

I smiled with gratitude when the officer handed me $200, the money provided to prisoners the day they are released. I slipped into the clothes my mother had picked out and brought with her, and then I sat in a holding cell for four hours. The waiting was agonizing but an inconvenience compared to the fifteen years of my life I had spent in prison. When I finally walked out of that cell, I cried in my mother's arms and kissed my father's tear-stained face. For a moment, time seemed to stand still and all I experienced was the warmth of our embrace.

I was socially expelled at the age of eighteen, grew into a woman behind prison walls, and at thirty-three was rejoining the wider world. Suddenly, the barbed-wire fencing was behind me. Gone were the shapeless pants and shirts that we all wore every day and the subordinate demeanor we adopted to survive in prison. Now people were looking me in the eye, as they would anyone else they encountered.

In those first few days of freedom I was flooded with memories and bombarded with sights and sensations that were incredible to me given the sterile environment in prison. My brain was in overdrive, taking it all in. Psychological ecstasy and emotional intoxication—that's my standard way of describing what it's like to come home after serving fifteen years in prison.

Being free created a surge of euphoria. To say I felt I had wings and could fly would be an understatement; I felt I had wings of steel that could carry me through a tornado. In other words, anything seemed possible. The knowledge that one day I would go home had been enough to motivate me to become a much better version of myself long before I was released, so I had years of accumulated ideas, dreams, and goals. I knew I couldn't do everything at once, but my spirit was energized and I wanted to go, go, go.

Within seventy-two hours, that feeling of euphoria was quieted by all that I needed to begin a new life: an ID, new clothes, a sustainable source of income that would allow me to buy my own food and have a home of my own. I also needed some serious time-management skills. I no longer had a prison schedule that dictated when to get up, when and where to report to work, when to eat, and when to sleep. A day in the free world had so much time to fill and yet I often underestimated how long it would take to do something.

Because I had served a lengthy prison sentence, I was required to complete a residential reentry program as a condition of my parole. Unfortunately, the only program in the Bay Area, where I had lived and planned to make a life again, that had space for me was essentially a drug and alcohol treatment program. I didn't have a substance abuse problem and, ironically, as a certified drug and alcohol counselor I could have been teaching the classes I was required to attend thirty-plus hours every week.

Initially, I didn't realize I was being institutionalized yet again. I was still too absorbed in and grateful for my freedom to recognize this so-called reentry program wasn't set up to help me actually rejoin the community. There, as in most other transitional housing facilities, everyone follows the same routine, and freedom and responsibility are doled out in increments incompatible with the rhythms and demands of normal life.

I had to turn down several job opportunities because I wasn't allowed to work until my fourth month in the program. I renewed my driver's license two weeks after coming home but wasn't allowed to drive throughout the entire seven months I was in the program. But the most frustrating aspects for me were the rules that restricted how much time

I could spend with my family. I saw my loving parents more when I was in prison.

As I had done for so many years, I swallowed the irritations and stayed focused on taking care of my body, mind, and spirit and preparing for my future. I knew this too would end. Also, as a woman of color I recognized that programs like this one provided a safety net that kept many women who looked like me from becoming a homeless statistic. I had a family that would have taken me in; many women and men leaving prison have no one waiting with open arms. Still, in the back of my mind I couldn't help but think society could do better. I even imagined what that might look like.

Today, I'm helping to create the kind of support I once dreamed of—an approach to reentry housing that actually helps formerly incarcerated people build a life in the community. Since August 2018, the Homecoming Project that I manage has been matching individuals who have transformed themselves over many years in prison, with residents of Alameda County who have a spare room in their home available for up to six months and want to be part of someone's successful reentry.[1]

The men and women who are selected to participate in the Homecoming Project have less than a one percent risk of committing a new crime according to an objective assessment conducted by the California Department of Parole.[2] They are highly motivated and ready to succeed but don't have a home to return to. Family and friends who might have welcomed and sheltered them have moved on with their lives, left the city, or even passed away.

We undertake a thorough process to pair hosts and participants who are compatible in terms of living preferences—early birds versus night owls, smokers and not, those who love to cook, women who are only comfortable hosting other women, the role of faith in a person's life, etc. We consider a slew of objective factors and go further to ensure that the individuals we pair meaningfully connect on a personal level. Both parties have to agree to the match. That careful process builds trust from the beginning.

Instead of collecting rent, the Homecoming Project pays hosts directly: $25 a day, paid monthly. Hosts also receive an up-front payment of $250 to cover any expenses associated with preparing the participant's room and normal wear and tear on their home. Financial compensation for hosts is a core aspect of the project: through the sharing economy we're able to assist people leaving prison and also channel dollars to individuals and families in cities that are becoming less and less affordable.

By temporarily lifting the burden of finding and paying for housing in an expensive real estate market, the Homecoming Project provides a base from which formerly incarcerated people can begin to build a new life. But we provide more than just housing. Each participant works one-on-one with a professional navigator employed by the Homecoming Project. Together they develop a personal reentry plan that identifies goals and the tasks required to make progress toward those goals. Goals range, for example, from finding a particular type of employment, to becoming part of a faith community, to regaining custody of children. To increase the odds of success, we partner with an array of community-based organizations that provide specific services and supports. Toward the end of the six months, we help people find a long-term place to live—a challenge aided by the fact that when they're applying for a room to rent or for their own apartment, they have a reference from their host that speaks to their character and responsibility.

While our supportive services are focused on participants, our staff also work with new hosts to help them understand the challenges people face after a lengthy period of incarceration and are available to answer questions or address a host's concerns at any point. Dinner and conversation sessions, held every other month and open to all hosts, provide opportunities for them to learn more and experience the support and enthusiasm of their peers—a host community that is slowly growing in number.

When I first met London, her voice quivered as she asked me how to apply. Her fear of becoming homeless was palpable, but I remember seeing more in her eyes than sheer desperation. This was a young woman who didn't want to disappoint anyone, perhaps especially herself. And I saw hope in her smile when I tried to lighten the discussion of a very heavy topic: where would she lay her head down in a month's time?

In "Nowhere to Go: Homelessness Among Formerly Incarcerated People," Lucius Couloute of the Prison Policy Initiative writes that people who have served a prison sentence are nearly ten times more likely to be homeless than the general public.[3] Aside from the particular and often unfair barriers that a person with a criminal record faces, the truth is that anyone starting over in life—and that's exactly what someone who's been incarcerated for years or decades has to do—will have a bundle of burdens to lift and obstacles to overcome. Yet the systems we've created to help them often make the transition harder.

London was no exception. After serving a fourteen-year sentence, she was released to a halfway house that, much like the facility where I was placed, restricted her freedom and thus hampered her ability to make a new life for herself. Even worse, she was about to lose the only home she had because of changes to the facility's eligibility criteria—something that often accompanies a shift in funding. Even her parole agent's hands were tied. I have no doubt that without our help London would have become homeless, her dreams along with her belongings on the streets of Oakland.

I quickly learned that the frightened woman I initially encountered was actually a charismatic person with ambition, talent, and enormous potential. We matched London with Sophia in December 2018. A week after she moved in, London found a job as a policy fellow at a nonprofit that works with prisoners' legal issues. Since then she has been filmed as part of a documentary series, was featured on the local news station, and is currently a local radio host.[4] A safe and welcoming home in the community, not apart from it in yet another facility, unlocked London's potential. "Being in the program saved me," she says.

When I met Eddie, he was sleeping each night in whatever safe place he could find, storing his few belongings at a twenty-four-hour gym, and showering at the gym in the morning to arrive at work clean—that's how much he valued the culinary job he found after prison. Eddie had no family to help him. "Everyone died while I was inside," he told me.

Like London, he initially had a bed in a transitional facility that he suddenly lost. His spirit was strong and he worked hard, but he didn't have the right kind of support to get ahead of the economic curve. After learning about the Homecoming Project, Eddie's parole officer contacted us on his behalf.

Wanting to appear strong and self-sufficient, Eddie was initially reluctant to admit he was homeless and to accept our help, but he came to trust us. We matched him with Terri. A longtime Oakland resident, Terri had been opening her home to community members in need for over ten years, so becoming a Homecoming Project host was a natural decision for her, and when she opened her door to Eddie she'd already had a successful hosting experience through us.

When you're starting at or near the bottom, it's a beautiful feeling when someone gives you a ladder on which to climb up. The process of coming home is unique to each person, so we support people as they find their own way up that ladder. Eddie is now stable instead of existing in survival mode. Not only is he taking care of himself, he's giving back to the community that supported him by volunteering at a local food bank.

As hosts welcome formerly incarcerated people into their homes and introduce them to friends and neighbors, and they in turn give something back to the community, a form of restorative justice occurs that is meaningful to everyone involved.

I knew from the beginning there were empty bedrooms in Oakland that could provide a home base for people making the difficult transition from prison to the free world. I knew it could be safe for everyone, and I knew that six months of free housing in the right environment would make all the difference to someone starting over in life. What I didn't anticipate was the extent to which our hosts would mentor, guide by example, and inspire the people they welcomed into their homes. Our hosts are serving as powerful role models and conveying important life skills just by being themselves. To be in the presence every day of someone living a healthy and productive life and overcoming the challenges life presents to all of us turns out to be enormously beneficial for formerly incarcerated people.

We've built a model of reentry housing and support that at scale will be less expensive than the transitional housing facilities that don't work. Our model also puts money in the hands of people, stimulating the economy at the grassroots level, instead of lining the pockets of the mostly for-profit corporations that run transitional housing facilities. The challenges we're facing are not unique to Alameda County. All over the country, people coming home from prisons are being forced to the margins of their communities. From California and Texas to Florida and New York, people coming out of prison are met with inadequate or nonexistent housing services and all too often their only option is to sleep on the street. The barriers are even greater for people in the transgender community, who are often barred from accessing transitional housing that matches their gender identity. Similarly, many transitional housing programs exclude people who were serving long-term sentences, often for violent convictions.

I've been gifted with watching my community embrace people that society once expelled, and through the community's support and encouragement, watching those individuals blossom into the incredible people I'm proud to know and serve. They've become co-workers, members of local church congregations, the electrician you call, a favorite radio host, the volunteer at your neighborhood food pantry, friends, neighbors, and family members to confide in and rely on.

It is past time that states across the country recognize that the current approach to transitional housing doesn't do enough to serve people's needs. Policy makers must do more to ensure that people are returning to safe housing that will provide them with opportunities to rebuild their lives upon release. Instead of investing in privately funded organizations that are profiting off of people, policy makers must focus their resources on approaches like the Homecoming Project that are clearly demonstrating an ability to meet the needs of people of all walks who are returning to their communities after incarceration. What I bring to the work from my own experience coming home after many years in prison, along with my drive to change peoples' lives for the better, carries me forward. My heart swells, I smile wide and often cry when I witness people genuinely connecting across their very different life experiences. And when someone who has spent what feels like a lifetime in prison finally gets a set of wings, we exchange a certain look, a shared understanding that they can indeed fly.

12

"Life" Means Death

Reginald Manning

Reginald Manning was born and raised in Baltimore, Maryland. He's been incarcerated in the Maryland Department of Corrections since 2003. Manning is passionate about youth advocacy and writing, and his first book, a novel called Bullets and Black Roses, *is set for publication in 2020. Manning writes, "My life's mission is to transcend the ignorance of my past and live a life of positive reform." He discusses possible changes to Maryland's parole process.*

I'm serving a life sentence—with seventy-five years tacked onto the back of it for good measure. Realistically, my making a plea for lifers to get parole, even if heard, probably won't affect my situation. Even so, I speak now to those who would listen, with the hope that somebody's future may look more appealing than mine. What makes a person irredeemable? What level of wickedness must one reach before society marks one unfit for civilization? I've asked myself those questions a lot during the first sixteen years of my incarceration.

The answer changes often, mostly depending on the depth of either my honesty or acceptance on any given day.

At the beginning, one of the hardest things about prison was learning the undesirable truths about myself. For the first few years of my life sentence, I was numb. It was like a part of me had sequestered itself inside some fortified place within me. I viewed my new life, my living situation, the men confined with me all from the hollowness of that fortified place. It was like I was on autopilot. My smiles were manufactured, my conversations were empty, my movements had no purpose. Really, the only words that seemed to register in my brain were the ones that the judge spoke when he sentenced me: "Life with the possibility of parole." What did that even mean? It sounded like some twisted oxymoron.

Since 1995, when then governor of Maryland Parris N. Glendening declared, "Life means life," the Maryland Parole Commission has been powerless to grant parole to any person serving a life sentence, even if they meet the criteria.[1] So despite the fact that a person may be sentenced to life with the possibility of parole, people serving life sentences in Maryland learn fairly quickly that in reality, that possibility essentially doesn't exist. In fact, "life" means death.

It's neither fiscally nor socially responsible to warehouse lifers in cases where rehabilitation is possible. Taxpayers have blindly paid the bill to keep the cogs of America's prison machine well-oiled. Splintered families and fractured communities are just some of the effects of mass incarceration without rehabilitation. Mahatma Gandhi is attributed as saying that the root of violence is "wealth without work, pleasure without conscience, knowledge without character, commerce without morality, science without humanity, worship without sacrifice, and politics without principles."[2] As I've established the principles by which I govern myself, I've often reflected on the principles we hold uniformly as a nation. I understand the desire to keep violent criminals off the streets. However, I do wish to pose this simple question: Can people change? What if we applied the same sympathetic standards by which we judge ourselves to our judgment of others?

Allow me a minute to bare my soul. I'm guilty of taking a man's life. I've never denied this fact, even at my trial. It's easy to look at that one moment of my life and try to encapsulate my entire being within it. That moment, no matter how visceral, no matter how long-lasting the effects, was one of many. A shard of time, linked to the many other moments before and after it that begin to reveal the tapestry of my life.

That moment links back to another moment when, at seven years old, I came home to find my mother's boyfriend dead from an overdose in our apartment's bathroom. The trauma of that moment connects to my years spent watching my mother use the same poison that killed him, and to finally understanding that she was an addict as well. It connects to my history of being bullied for being too afraid and too small to fight. I took many beatings before I fought back, and a lot more before I won. It connects to my first lessons in violence and the many nights I was awakened by the sound of gunfire outside my project window. It connects to my memories of all the blaring sirens and screams. It connects to my discoveries of the aftermath of those crimes, walking to school as a child past yellow tape and dead bodies covered with sheets. It connects to my awareness that people do awful things to each other.

It connects to an echo of the weekly announcements made over my middle school's intercom—that's how they notified us that one of our peers had been murdered. The first time I heard one of those announcements, I was shocked. By the twentieth time, I was jaded. My history of trauma showed itself in my longtime belief that I would die young. It showed itself in my delinquency. My first stint in juvenile detention was for grand theft auto. I was handcuffed and put in a cell. Almost all of my friends had been through the same—the system was our training ground. The moment of my crime connects to and stems from my early acclimation to bondage.

That moment also connects to the first time I stared down the barrel of a gun. I was twelve, at the mercy of my faceless assailant. He wanted the proceeds from the nights I spent trafficking drugs. I gave them to him, but he shot me anyway. The fact of my crime is linked to those moments that left me wanting a gun of my own. Do you see the picture that I'm trying to paint? Many things have to happen to bring a person to the point where they can stand before another with violent intent.

Learning the undesirable truths about myself was the hardest part of prison for me. I learned that I'd tricked myself into believing that, because I had a rough life, any harm I did to others was just me playing the hand I was dealt. I know that wasn't the case. I'd lost myself to negativity and gave up my power to my environment. Even still, I made a choice—misguided, but a choice nonetheless.

Emotions and experiences, choices and consequences—we all relate to these things. We've all done bad things, and in some way, whether intentionally or unintentionally, mentally or physically, we will hurt someone at some point in the course of our lives. The conscious among us will learn from our mistakes and do better. Now, in no way do I wish to minimize the crime of murder, or its impact. Nor do I believe that every person who comes to prison has the desire or the capability to change. All I'm saying is that some in my situation use their time to transform themselves for the better. In those cases, when the possibility of parole was included in their sentences, parole should be realistically considered.

Maryland is one of three U.S. states that require the governor to sign off on the parole of inmates serving life sentences.[3] Since Glendening's stance on parole and life sentences was adopted as policy in 1994, no Maryland governor until Governor Larry Hogan (who has approved two cases as of this writing) has signed off on parole for a lifer.[4] I believe that this policy should be thoroughly reevaluated, and corrected by legislation that places parole power for everyone back into the hands of the state's Parole Commission.

One of the biggest obstacles I see with that endeavor is community support. I would like to see us work to bridge the gap between prisoners and the public. Statistically speaking, short-term offenders often become long-term offenders, or lifers themselves. This reveals to us that something is happening to cause people in so many cases to gradually get worse between the their first and last offense. Prison for so many has become the inevitable final destination.

I believe that this sense of resignation can be changed. In service to that cause, I propose the creation of Link Ledgers, a screened online forum where victims and prisoners can post accounts of their experiences. The mission of the site would be to "Link" people affected by crime by creating a place for victims to record the accounts of their experiences, while viewing the open and honest Ledgers of the convicted. This would be an effort to allow repentant inmates to communicate and express remorse and explain the events that led them to their offenses. It would also be a place where victims could seek answers and healing. Oftentimes victims carry with them unseen scars from their experiences, and they yearn to be understood on a human level, outside of the criminal-victim dynamic. The conversation could occur under different headings such as "I want to know why . . ." and "I did it because . . ." No excuses, just honest accounts of lives and the effects of choices.

I think such a forum would go a long way toward combating the dehumanization of both victims and perpetrators. The goal would be not to condone but to understand, and then change. It's only through our shared awareness that we can erase ignorance. Maybe we can share the human Link between those affected by crime and those convicted of committing a crime through the sharing of our Ledgers. I know firsthand what it feels like to be both a victim and a victimizer. I also know that I found forgiveness through greater understanding. An unobscured look at my own life and experiences showed me that I was capable of causing the same type of pain that others had caused me. This insight forced me to see myself and others on a human level and to acknowledge that we have the capacity to harm, but also the ability to heal and find redemption.

I was a damaged person who did destructive things. My actions affected people in ways I'll probably never fully comprehend. I took a man's life, and I have to live with the shame and regret of that knowledge every day. Whatever the choices I made as a teen and a young adult, I'd never make them again as a thirty-eight-year-old person. My sentence included the possibility of parole because the judge believed me capable of change, and I have changed. With the system the way it is, lifers with parole in Maryland are no different than lifers without parole. If that's the case, why make the distinction? I believe that it's our connection to, rather than our isolation from, one another that will reform our prison system. I know that change is possible: I live it, and parole is the doorway at the end of the transition. It should be opened for those who prove themselves worthy.

13

The 13th and the Problem of the Color Line

Mika'il DeVeaux, PhD

Professor DeVeaux was formerly incarcerated and is currently a lecturer at Nassau Community College, part of the SUNY system. He is the co-founder and executive director of Citizens Against Recidivism, Inc., directs the Muslim Reentry Initiative, and is a certified anger management facilitator. Dr. DeVeaux is also the founder and principal at DeVeaux Association, a consulting firm that provides evaluation, monitoring, and other services for nonprofits. He discusses the 13th Amendment and its relevance across every aspect of justice reform.

The framers of the U.S. Constitution knew all along that the 13th Amendment was written to address one concern: "the problem of the color line." That problem, as articulated by W.E.B. DuBois, speaks simultaneously to the historical relationship between people of African descent and the United States, the systematic effort to destroy Afrocentric notions of self, and the construction of a negative black identity.

I learned about my connection to the 13th Amendment during the thirty-two years I spent under correctional supervision, which, according to a literal reading and interpretation of the amendment, made me a slave of the state. In every maximum-security prison where I was confined, I was forced to work mopping floors, mowing grass, or doing some other menial task until I figured out how to do other work that I felt was less demeaning. Even so, those changes were reminiscent of a slight adjustment in status. I had moved from being a slave in the field to one in the big house. Then I took "clerk jobs" that came with a few perks. For example, in some instances I was a chaplain's clerk and given an "institutional pass" that allowed me to move about the prison unescorted. On another occasion I became a clerk in the mess hall and had access to fresh vegetables, extra food, and regular showers. Rather than become complacent, I knew that I was still a slave and sought a much broader understanding about the context of my situation. I began to examine stories about the past to inform my contemporary analysis, thinking about what could be done to dismantle the foundation of the U.S. system of incarceration.

While in state prison I learned of the raw power of the state and its administrators. I arrived in state prison in 1979. In each prison I was confined—Sing Sing, Comstock, Clinton, Attica, Auburn, and others—I could still smell the smoke from the 1971 Attica riot and the stench of the dead bodies in the air. Day-to-day prison life experience was pathological. The conditions of confinement were emasculating, humiliating, and dehumanizing. I never envisioned the kind of suffering I would experience as a consequence of violating the law, nor did I think the treatment I received was compatible with the stated function of incarceration, the aims of rehabilitation, or the goal of positive social adjustment and service upon my expected return. I still cannot remember why I was surprised when they said, "Get in that cell, nigga." I did not find a justice system, but a modern iteration of an old, infamous system based solely upon the subjugation of a whole race of people, of which I happen to be a member.

Slavery and bondage have been thoroughly connected to "the new world." Since the fifteenth century, every European empire of the modern era has been enriched by the forced labor of African slaves in both Europe and the Americas. Each European competed with their neighbor for the right to traffic in African bodies to further their quest for wealth, industrial advances, and colonial enterprises. New language ushered in an ideology of white supremacy and the social construction of race, such that "white" connoted goodness, Christianity, and superiority; blackness, on the other hand, was demonized, made inferior and heathen, used to justify the idea that certain people deserved to be enslaved. Race-based slavery freed whites from guilt or shame, as blackness was conceptualized as something less than human.

Adopted in 1787, the Northwest Ordinance—all but forgotten today—detailed the process whereby lands of what were then northwest territories would be admitted into the Union as new states equal to the original thirteen, guaranteeing its inhabitants civil rights and, importantly, outlawing slavery. The "slavery clause" of the ordinance was a precursor to the 13th Amendment, adopted almost one hundred years later:

Article 6 of the Northwest Ordinance, July 13, 1787: There shall be neither slavery nor involuntary servitude in the said territory, otherwise than in the punishment of crimes whereof the party shall have been duly convicted.

Section 1 of the 13th Amendment to the U.S. Constitution, December 6, 1865: Neither slavery nor involuntary servitude, except as a punishment for crime whereof the party shall have been duly convicted, shall exist within the United States, or any place subject to their jurisdiction.

Advocates of the 13th Amendment understood its design to "obliterate the last lingering vestiges of the slave system: its chattelizing, degrading, and bloody codes; its dark, malignant, and barbarizing spirit; all it was and is; everything connected to it or pertaining to it."[1]

What is clear now is that the passage of the 13th Amendment in its present form had some but not all of the expected impact that African Americans anticipated would follow, despite the intentions of its framers. Frederick Douglass declared that the passage of the amendment was just the beginning of the fight. Responding to an attempt by William Lloyd Garrison to disband the American Anti-Slavery Society after the passage of the 13th Amendment, Douglass prophesized that the objectives of the abolitionist movement would not be completed so long as whites "retained in their hands power to exclude [people of African descent] from political rights." Douglass went on to predict that black people would be "reduced to a condition similar to slavery. They would not call it slavery, but some other name," and warned that "all of us had better wait and see what new form this old monster will assume, in what new skin this old snake will come forth."[2]

Despite a fundamental change in the law, Southern whites were not yet ready to change the master-slave social relationship they previously held that defined what it meant to be white. The Black Codes, Vagrancy Laws, Pig Laws, and other legislation à la the 13th Amendment were designed and used post–Emancipation Proclamation specifically against African Americans to facilitate their incarceration for slave-like work, convict leasing, and other forms of forced labor in an attempt to make up for the lost economic benefits of free labor enjoyed during slavery.

The reconfigured judicial system ushered in a new relationship between African Americans and law enforcement. Sheriffs, deputies, and some court officials derived most of their compensation from fees charged to black people convicted of crimes for each step in their arrest, conviction, and assignment to private companies. These efforts gained wide support from a populace looking to control and punish what Michael Hallet called the first American "'black crime problem' . . . with total disregard for the economically destitute position in which freed slaves found themselves after the war . . . trying to feed themselves and looking for shelter."[3]

Matters were not helped by the passage of the Civil Rights Act of 1866. Its wording was yet another mouthful of hollow pronouncements that whites were unable to live up to in the face of black freedom, and it did nothing to halt white people's efforts to maintain the notion of slavery by another name.

According to the act, rights enjoyed by white citizens would be afforded to all "without regard to any previous condition of slavery or involuntary servitude, except as a punishment for crime whereof the party shall have been duly convicted."[4]

Past policies that racialized crime or criminalized blackness before the commission of crime have broad implications for today's system of hyper-incarceration and the post-release experiences of black men. Displays of Confederate battle flags in penal institutions and police stations, police killings of unarmed black men and women, questions about equal citizenship status of African Americans and other people of color, and acts that fail to recognize their humanity continue to be part of the status quo.

Apart from the correctional system, social environments that are polarized by race undermine individuals' successful integration post-prison. The direct and collateral consequences of former incarceration make it, in the words of Brett E. Garland, Cassia Spohn, and Eric J. Wodahl, "hard to deny that racial disparity in imprisonment poses a serious threat to the perception and reality of the full integration of Blacks into American society."[5]

Today, as in the postbellum era, the past is the present: slaves laws became Black Codes, plantations became prisons, slave labor became prison labor; today, the criminal justice system and all that it entails has become a racialized system of crime control "without ever referring to race." Current incarceration data show that people in state or federal custody are more likely to be people of color (71 percent males, 53 percent females) than white (29 percent males, 47 percent females).[6]

In its present form, the 13th Amendment includes an obvious legislative loophole that provides the means to continue, in a legal way, the institution of slavery, in which federal and state governments, rather than private citizens, are the official and sanctioned slaveholders. Before the enactment of this law, the U.S. economy had a significant agricultural base bolstered by free slave labor. In this era of neo-slavery, the state and its corporate partners—including Abbott Laboratories, AT&T, AutoZone, Bank of America, Bayer, Cargill, Caterpillar, Chevron, Conagra, Costco, Eli Lilly, GlaxoSmithKline, International Paper, John Deere, Johnson & Johnson, Koch Industries, Mary Kay, McDonald's, Merck, Motorola, Pfizer, Sears, Starbucks, United Airlines, UPS, Verizon, Wendy's, Whole Foods, and others—have colluded to exploit prison labor and form what some call the prison industrial complex.[7]

I would argue that to be worthy of serious consideration, any policy approach seeking to address any aspect of the justice system, including the problem of reentry, must include in its analysis mention of the 13th Amendment and a call to challenge it as it currently stands. Using the 13th Amendment as a focal point, policy discussions must begin with the acknowledgment that the U.S. prison system is a slave-based system according to the U.S. Constitution, and that it is a tool of state-sanctioned punishment incompatible with any of the supposed traditional functions of punishment generally associated with imprisonment: reformation (or rehabilitation), incapacitation, retribution, and deterrence.

Moreover, any honest analysis should draw attention to and question the use of private prisons. It is necessary to ask whether private prisons that compete for a share of the prison market are in the best interest of taxpayers, the government, and those housed in those prisons for the purpose of "rehabilitation"—or whether, like slavery, such prisons have been established to generate profit off black and brown bodies.

Efforts to amend the 13th Amendment by abolishing its punishment clause can achieve several important outcomes, including the following:

1. a critical chance for the public to be made aware of the ongoing violation of human and constitutional rights that the punishment clause makes possible, and its consequences for the future of racial and economic democracy in America;
2. an understanding of the devastating consequences that the expropriation of human labor by the U.S. carceral state has had and continues to have on the economic and political development (and underdevelopment) of black and brown communities;
3. an opportunity to change the conversation about our country's punitive prison policies and the abolition of the U.S. system of punishment as we know it; and
4. an opportunity to establish a truth and reconciliation commission to begin steps toward national healing.

Let us begin that work now.

14

From the Ground Up:
Tapping the Strengths of Incarcerated People

Mathew Lucas Ayotte

At the time of his submission, Mathew Lucas Ayotte was incarcerated in a state prison in Maine, where he was enrolled as a student at the University of Maine at Augusta. Ayotte has earned his associate's degree in liberal studies and is earning credits toward a bachelor's degree in an interdisciplinary degree program in mental health counseling, addiction studies, and restorative justice. Currently he is finishing a federal sentence at a United States Penitentiary in Arizona, where he facilitates meditation and yoga classes. He proposes the creation of strengths-based peer mentorship programs within institutions and prisons.

Peer-to-peer mentorship is an integral part of humanizing the criminal justice system because it encourages and empowers the people most affected by the experience of incarceration—those who are serving the time. If men and women were afforded the opportunity to share their life experiences in whatever area of specialization or expertise they might have, the result would be to the mutual benefit of all involved. In this way, inmates' senses of self would be bolstered instead of diminished.

We all have roles and various skills that make up a sense of who we are. Whether it be a career role or family role, everyone has a way of identifying themselves within the scope of the world in which they live. Often it's these very roles that provide us our sense of worth. What happens when these roles are stripped from us? How does the stay-at-home mom cope when her incarceration keeps her from being home with her children? How does the stonemason make sense of his days when he sits idle staring out the window of a prison cell? Problems such as these are not addressed. Although there might be programs available for incarcerated persons to participate in, they are typically not focused on addressing this loss of identity.

Incarceration is a dehumanizing experience. Upon arrest you are manacled, placed in handcuffs—sometimes shackles are used to secure your person, and they are often connected to the handcuffs by a belly chain. Once you are in custody, the intake process begins. You are photographed and fingerprinted, stripped naked and made to dance the most inhumane version of the hokey-pokey imaginable. Next you are given a uniform that never fits correctly, with bold lettering signifying that you are an inmate or prisoner. By this point, your sense of self has been thoroughly undermined. You are then given a number that takes precedent over your name. If your name is used at all, it is your last name. In every way your identity has been reframed from the moment you were arrested. So who are you now?

Perhaps you know sign language, maybe you were an educator. Maybe you were a carpenter and a business owner. These are transferable skills, important sources of expertise that can be tapped to facilitate a process of growth in an environment where idleness and boredom too often spawn self-destructive behaviors. During the screening process, the assessment of an individual should address their unique gifts and talents and their willingness to focus on them. Then a more proactive experience could be developed as a way to prepare incarcerated individuals for reintegrating into society with new skills and, for those who share their expertise, to develop in them a more positive sense of self-worth.

Thanks to a progressive administration at the Maine State Prison, I was afforded the opportunity to participate in and facilitate a peer-to-peer mentoring program; these programs included meditation and yoga classes, cognitive behavioral courses, hospice volunteer work, religious and spiritual groups, and, most importantly, secondary education opportunities that bolstered my confidence and led me to direct my life toward a path of service. I have witnessed firsthand the benefit of peer-driven programs, and I am convinced of the profound difference such person-to-person service work can make for an individual.

It has been my good fortune to have the opportunity to participate in the Second Chance Pell Grant program, which provides individuals with funding to take college courses while incarcerated.[1] Of course there are numerous factors that must be considered and many rules that must be adhered to, but it is a program that is currently being successfully piloted across the country.

When I began my course work via the Second Chance Pell Grant, I was thirty-nine years old. It had been twenty years since I had been expelled from my first university experience because of my first conviction for a crime. That this opportunity came to me full circle did not escape my notice, and I committed myself to the work ahead of me. One of the main factors that led me to get involved with the Pell program was the encouragement from other men in the many other programs available to me who positively influenced my decisions and encouraged me to apply. Thanks to support from them and the facility's educational staff, I applied and was admitted into the programs I thought best suited to my personality and interests.

It has been just shy of two years since I began my degree path, and I have one course requirement remaining before I will earn my associate's degree in liberal arts. I currently have a 3.89 GPA and am planning for the possibility of working in the human services field. This would have never occurred to me without the encouragement of my friends and colleagues. Their support allowed me to apply myself to a course of study in which I was able to excel. In doing so I developed a more positive sense of self-worth, one that afforded me the courage and wherewithal to share my good fortunes with others. I began tutoring other students and helping out the education staff. I found purpose and meaning in my days, meeting my peers and professors with humility and gratitude for the opportunity at hand. The most rewarding realization came when my professors interacted with me as their equals. It was at this point that I was able to recognize the transformation I had undergone.

As I pursued my college degree, I got involved in a yoga teacher training course offered at the facility where I was incarcerated. As this had been a lifelong interest of mine, I was thrilled to take part. However, in looking back and being honest with myself, I wonder whether I would have had the confidence to sign up if the college courses I had been taking hadn't raised my spirits significantly. I doubt I would have volunteered to teach classes and facilitate meditation and tai chi classes. In these moments I was given the unique gift of working with the hearts and minds of my peers, in a place where it is common to hold oneself close and resist being vulnerable. Instead, I got to be present for many breakthroughs and revelations. Never in my life would my eyes have been opened to the power of self-reflection were it not for the opportunities that paved the way for me to heal.

In addition to my yoga teacher training, I grew close to the hospice workers who attended to me. Although I previously knew each of the men doing service, after being in closer contact I saw another side of them, a deeper, more empathetic side. This experience moved me to volunteer for Personal Support Specialist certification, where I would work with the ill and elderly, especially at end-of-life providing palliative care. Through this training, I received an education covering a range of areas, from the art of being present, to strategies for establishing boundaries, to care techniques for persons with disabilities. This kind of service work was never even a thought in my mind before I began the journey of pursuing my college degree once again. Because I took one step forward onto a path of education, I grew to have a sense of responsibility and accountability to my fellow man and the whole of humanity, which I was never quite mindful enough to feel before.

The most powerful experience of all was having the opportunity to facilitate the Psychology of Incarceration program created by Khalil Osirus, a formerly incarcerated individual. The program is based on a cognitive behavioral therapy approach, which addresses one's thinking and perception of things. In the two years that I led this program, I worked with over 250 men, witnessing the effect of psychological empowerment, which taught that if you can think your way into prison, you can also think your way out. I adapted Osirus's framework and incorporated the concept that you have the choice of living by one of two sets of "ABCs"—either Actions + Behaviors = Consequences, or Actions + Behaviors = Choices. The difference between one ABC set and the other was that of *reacting* to situations and circumstances or *responding* to them.

Something so simple had a considerable impact on the lives of the men I had the honor and pleasure of helping along their journeys to self-discovery. In hindsight, I see myself as possibly benefiting the most from my involvement in this work, although the men I worked with often thanked me and came to me for advice on matters in their lives. I benefited greatly from being given the space to hone my teaching skills and develop my speaking voice, craft my teaching style, and manage a group of individuals while presenting material and keeping it interesting. I remember a class where I admitted to the men that all my life I had wanted to do exactly what it was I was doing, but I had not been able to do it until I came to prison. Outside of prison, I wasn't able to get out of my own way long enough to care about other individuals. It was because of my experiences in prison that I have grown into the service-oriented man of compassion that I am today. How very humbling this precious gift has been.

I share these experiences because it was my privilege to observe how effective personal mentorship can be, especially within a carceral environment, which popular culture depicts as a place of violence and disregard for individual well-being, a place devoid of love and safety, where one can't help feeling like a stranger among strangers. You might wonder what it is like to enter into a cold, dark, steel-barred world where everyone is at the lowest point in their lives. When you are surrounded by such desperation and helplessness, an unfortunate way of protecting oneself from being vulnerable is to embody the stereotypes we too often see in the media of the hard-edged, musclebound, menacing convict. But how does taking on the characteristics of such a character affect the individual behind the mask? Can they just turn off the "bad dude" persona? What sort of person will be released back into society when all is said and done—the original human or the new character? There are facilities here in the U.S. where those who enter do not exit except in a body bag. This is a reality many Americans are not conscious of, but it is one we can actively protect and safeguard against by focusing on a more humane approach to corrections.

This approach begins with understanding that every

human being is worthy and deserving of respect. When, as is so often the case, an individual is at their lowest low because they are in prison, there is no reason to degrade them any further. It is not the responsibility of the correctional staff to punish those serving time. The sentence is the punishment. I believe the premise of prison should be changed to one of rehabilitation with a focus on a strength-based perspective. The correctional staff should take an individual's interests and life experiences into consideration, in a concerted effort to embolden that person's spirit, with the aim of encouraging them to overcome the odds and not return to whatever behavior led them to becoming incarcerated.

What if men and women were given the opportunity to share their niche knowledge with others who are incarcerated? Would people without skills benefit from learning new skills? What might be accomplished if the skills of each and every incarcerated person were drawn upon rather than suppressed? In the U.S. today, more than two million men, women, and juveniles are behind bars.[2] How many of these people have something to offer the world? The answer, of course, is all of them. Every one of these people is worthwhile and deserves the opportunity to share with the world what is lying dormant within them, what is just waiting to be coaxed and teased out of them.

Peer-to-peer mentorship is a means of accomplishing this process by supporting the gifts and talents of incarcerated persons, thereby creating an environment of openness and relationships centered on mutual respect. This is the antithesis of what currently exists in the justice system, where an us-versus-them attitude is perpetuated to everyone's detriment. It does not serve society to marginalize and subject our own citizens to a rigorous stripping away of personhood.

The former professional boxer Mike Tyson relates how his first manager implanted in him a sense of invincibility, of greatness. This won Tyson the heavyweight title at a young age. But when he went to prison, was stripped naked and given a number, the dehumanizing effect paralyzed him. It paralyzes most of the unfortunate folks who have had the experience of serving time.[3]

Instead, we should embrace an approach of elevating the already-broken spirit to a higher ground, a moral ground, upon which a person who has done something wrong can stand firm in society as a citizen, repentant of wrongs committed, but not shamed into believing that they themselves are in some way bad. There is a difference between guilt and shame. Guilt is knowing that you did something wrong and feeling sorry for it. Shame is believing that you are bad and that there is something wrong with you as a person that can't be fixed. With a little time and attention, almost anything can be fixed.

How might a peer-to-peer initiative work? First, I think the general attitude toward incarceration and the criminal justice system would have to be revamped to reflect a more informed picture, one that acknowledges that the United States is the world's most incarcerated nation, and asks why that is. I alone cannot make this policy change, but in my own way, within my own sphere of influence, I can do my part. If individuals who are incarcerated are encouraged to do their part, that would be a significant step on the road to rehabilitating our criminal justice system—whether that involves someone using the sign language they know to help convey a deaf person's needs to an officer, or using their knowledge as an accountant to create a monthly budget for someone else to help them manage their disability check. With so many unanswered questions and needs and such a shortage of prison staff, the conditions of inmates' lives are often ignored until things reach a boiling point or the urgency fades forever. In either of these cases, a disservice is being done, not only to the individual in need, but also to society. Wouldn't it be simpler to authorize those who are willing to give their help to do just that?

Reform bills and progressive legislation address some of the more entrenched aspects of our criminal justice system, while matters such as how an incarcerated person spends the twenty-four hours of his or her day—idly sitting locked in a cell or doing community service work, two diametric approaches—have largely been unaddressed. I believe a majority of people would voluntarily give their time and energy to be productive, both to feel good about themselves and to be tired enough just to get a full night's sleep. What if such persons were allotted a wage? A job is getting done. Considering that we are still citizens, where does it say we cannot be paid a fair wage for our work?

This is a matter of taking advantage of available resources and not doing so in an exploitive way. There are programs where incarcerated persons are paid for their work, and there are other instances where that work is not compensated in a fair and honorable way. Consider the California firefighters who get paid one dollar a day for saving their state government millions.[4] This is not right, but it does show the initiative of incarcerated people. Those men and women are not doing the job because of the money, but they are putting their lives on the line for nothing more than the sense of giving back and doing the right thing. That has everything to do with dignity, and that is what peer-to-peer service cultivates and nurtures in those who partake in the experience.

We as a nation cannot ignore the disparity between the rich and the poor, the free and incarcerated, the haves and have-nots. It is a disparity that should not exist, because we are ultimately in this together. As many of us have already realized, what we do to another, we do to ourselves. I believe that we can change the system by getting involved, tapping the resources that are available to us, and implementing the age-old strategies of social capital and human investment theory. By supporting our fellow human beings, we *become* better human beings. This idea could have an exponential impact on the current criminal justice system by starting at the root, with the people who are serving time. Give each incarcerated person an outlet to express their best self, and I give my promise that our country would not regret it. The results would speak for themselves.

To anyone who reads this and finds themselves wondering how such an initiative would look, I encourage them to volunteer, speak up and out, go to your local councilperson or member of Congress. Do your part, give what you can. While you're at it, let us do our part, and let us give what we have to give. The world needs every little bit of love it can get, and this is a way to bring love back into the lives of incarcerated people everywhere by allowing them to work with their peers and experience the joy of being shown even just a modicum of patience and compassion.

15

A Bridge to Employment

Michelle Jones

Michelle Jones is a third-year doctoral student in American Studies at New York University. Incarcerated for twenty years, Michelle used her academic platform to publish and present her research findings on the history of Indiana's women's prison and dispel notions of about the reach and intellectual capacity of justice-involved women. In 2015, she and others testified before the Indiana Joint Committee on Prisons, Corrections, and the Criminal Code on reentry program ideas. She is currently board chair of Constructing Our Future, a reentry alternative for women, created by incarcerated women in Indiana. She is a 2017–18 Beyond the Bars fellow, a 2017–18 Research Fellow at Harvard University, and a 2018–19 Ford Foundation Bearing Witness Fellow with Art for Justice. She proposes the creation of an education and federal employment program for incarcerated individuals, helping them pursue higher education while incarcerated and become employees of the state upon release.

During my twenty years of incarceration, I observed so many amazing brilliant women just languishing in prison. Having completed all available rehabilitative, therapeutic, and educational programs offered, and considered a valuable asset and not a threat to themselves or others, these women—in my opinion—did not need to be incarcerated. They were older, wiser, and mature women, usually convicted on violent crimes. We often wondered what the world on the outside would think of the fact that the prison was largely run by women convicted of murder, arson, and battery. Leaders in the Indiana Women's Prison community and positive stabilizing forces within the prison culture, these women kept the facility operating on an even keel.

Without them, prisons wouldn't function effectively. Employed in clerk positions in the library, law library, family preservation, recreation center, and on suicide watch in solitary confinement, they were also the tutors, assistant registrars, medical management assistants, production assistants in building trades, and cosmetology and printshop workers. These were skilled women, and everyone knew that could be counted on and trusted. They created and nurtured a culture that privileged service, community, and education over drama. It was because of them that IWP had more than one thousand regular volunteers. Women focused on service, community, and education, and they were the hands and minds behind Children's Day, Camp, Teen Day, Family Preservation Center, Poetry Slams, Liturgical Dance Programs, Indiana Canine Assistant Network, and more. They started initiatives like the One Net–One Life Mosquito Net Project, Outlast Her Competitions, and Recycle Now campaigns.

One of my friends, Cierra,* was a nurse prior to her incarceration. In prison, she was employed in the law library and in the chapel. She would conduct research and write sentence modifications, post-conviction relief petitions, even habeas corpus petitions for women in need. She worked tirelessly to represent the women. Cierra also worked in the chapel and was the first person religious volunteers saw when they came to visit. Her kindness and professionalism were well known. Cierra often led the planning and execution of religious services, choir, and special facility events throughout the prison. Cierra's sentence—originally death row—was commuted to twenty-plus years. She did all of her executed time and went home to a new life and family, but, like a lot of women, she struggled to secure employment and housing when she got home. She struggled emotionally and psychically with the change from being a key person who facilitated the effective operation of the prison, to a person whose gifts and talents were suddenly subsumed under the taint of criminality. After every rejection, Cierra somehow held together the tattered pieces of her consciousness and spirit and eventually persevered in securing a job, but not without loss. In many ways, the dream of her new life after prison was crushed by her many rejections.

Another friend, Della, spent six months struggling to find a place to live even though she had a full-time job. She struggled, after ten years of incarceration where she was a role model and leader to other gender nonconforming women in sports, choir, and education, in an outside world where

---

* Names have been changed throughout to protect identities.

no one would rent to her. She ended up living at the YWCA under less than favorable conditions. More importantly, each housing rejection exacted a psychic toll on her. She told me more than once that she felt that people wanted her to fail.

While incarcerated, LeAnne received a vocational education, an associate's degree, and a bachelor's degree, among many other achievements (published writer and leader) and accolades. Everyone sought her wisdom and guidance. After eighteen years of incarceration, she went home to live with her family, ready to start a new life. But LeAnne could not get a job with a living wage and benefits. Even with a bachelor's degree, she was denied by potential employers over and over again, due to the violent nature of her conviction. The fits and starts of seasonal employment and jobs where she was employed under the table with no benefits eventually eroded her stable mental state, and she started drinking. Today, after being home for only four years, she is still struggling and now with substance use, a habit she kicked nearly two decades ago.

Knowing how we as incarcerated women succeeded, in spite of the violent nature of the prison and the constant changes within the administration and facilitation of the prison, I began to imagine a better reentry outcome for women such as Cierra, Della, LeAnne, and myself. People involved in the criminal legal system are not disposable or surplus. We are mothers, fathers, sons, and daughters who deserve a real legitimate chance to stitch our lives together again. Once we are legitimately capable of doing so, we should have that opportunity. We need a redistribution of the gifts, skills, and talents that incarcerated people use each day to keep the prison industrial complex robust and thriving. We need a pathway home so that we can give back to ourselves, our families, and our communities. Our labor, creativity, and care represent the heart of what makes prisons function, and these can be deployed in the outside world as well.

A key in my imagining was not only to create a way in which to aid in the reentry efforts of formerly incarcerated people who have been separated from the job market for a significant number of years, but also to change the ways in which prison, legislative, and law enforcement officials, and those in the larger community, view the incarcerated and formerly incarcerated. Such a social change can happen only through relationship, and relationship can happen only in proximity. The formerly incarcerated need to be near, around, and about, in order to assert our humanity and demand a recognition of the same. There is no one shape to force the formerly incarcerated to fit into. Quite the contrary, we ask the community to acknowledge our readiness and to rise up and meet us with opportunity.

I propose the creation of a Government Employee Project (GEP) that would utilize existing agencies and money, but refashion and reallocate them to help formerly incarcerated people have a safer landing, including guaranteed housing and employment, upon release. The Government Employee Project would be an extensive education and reentry program wherein mid-to-long-term incarcerated people earn a two- or four-year college degree and real work experience as an employee for their state, upon return to the community. Working for the state and its various agencies would place formerly incarcerated women and men in direct proximity to lawmakers and highlights my argument that proximity is needed to build relationship. Lawmakers and other officials who see and think of monsters when they imagine incarcerated and formerly incarcerated people will be challenged by those women and men to rethink their beliefs.

Through GEP, formerly incarcerated people become eligible for early parole and employment by the state by taking advantage of the higher education program in their prisons. This idea is gleaned from the tradition in some African countries of paying for their countrymen's education in the United States in exchange for those countrymen agreeing to work for their native government for two years or more.[1] GEP combines the pursuit of a higher education while incarcerated (or earned prior to incarceration) with guaranteed employment and housing upon release. More importantly, it is a pathway for women and men serving (unnecessary) long sentences to be released early from prison.

Once an individual is on parole or probation, the state and community-based organizations would step up with resources and support. The rationale around this idea would be to redirect money currently used to warehouse incarcerated people into a program wherein paroled women and men earn a living wage, receive guaranteed housing (recovery or transitional), and are provided other forms of support. The project would offer a stable and safe transition from prison, including wrap-around services to the people in the project. Any combination of partnering between states and community-based organizations could be configured to meet the participant's needs.

Once employed, participants can provide for many of their own needs, and this, together with elimination of the daily costs of incarcerating them in prisons, will result in a significant reduction in costs to the state. It is contrary to my nature to talk about people in relation to cost savings because, as GEP shows, I'm most concerned about people and their quality of life, yet I am well aware that the economics of my idea will be scrutinized. Addressing the costs head-on will silence those would-be detractors, who would cry about costs and fail to help the people. These women and men who have consistently demonstrated their ability to lead, manage, and organize in prison would take those skills and do the same for themselves at home. GEP represents a pathway in which state actors can become a part of the solution to mass incarceration and not just the everlasting propagators of a broken system.

I believe that we incarcerate too often and too long. Prisons have become the primary way in which we dispose of so-called surplus populations, actively warehousing people who, given access to resources and opportunity, need not be incarcerated. I've seen many aging brilliant women in prison—who are not a threat to anyone—find meaning in their lives, but whose talents and skills would be better served in the world than in prison. Until the current system is dismantled and we reimagine how we deal with people who harm others, those captive within the carceral state are in need right now of meaningful options in legislation and programming to mediate the collateral consequences of coming into contact with the criminal legal system.[2]

According to the Lumina Foundation, "the country needs 60 percent of working-age Americans to hold college degrees, workforce certificates, and other marketable post-secondary credentials by 2025."[3] Higher education programs across the country prove the link between education and anti-recidivism, and such programs should be expanded for the benefit of the whole of society.

The basic principles of GEP are applicable in any state because the components are either the same or an equivalent. GEP could begin in those states and prisons that already have higher education in prison programs. And most importantly, many of the resources needed for GEP to flourish already exist. What is required is for those resources to be drawn together and organized to serve formerly incarcerated people more explicitly. Assuming GEP's success, prisons and states embracing GEP could be pioneers in the field of reentry by investing in people who have taken responsibility for their lives, served the majority of their sentence, and demonstrated their readiness and capabilities every day.

It is widely known and accepted among incarcerated people and prison staff that many mid-to-long-term incarcerated people have made necessary changes in conduct and attitude, and are useful and of service to the prison in which they reside. Creating an opportunity for those persons to succeed back in the community can help everyone rethink the point of extremely long prison sentences.

The point of GEP is to bring home those women and men who work each and every day to sustain the prison in which they are located, so they can sustain themselves, their own families, and their communities. It is grounded on the abolitionist foundation that we should at every opportunity reduce the power of the prison industrial complex to reproduce itself, while we simultaneously improve the quality of life of those currently incarcerated and formerly incarcerated.

16

Closing the Literacy Gap

Sreedhar Potarazu, MD

Dr. Sreedhar Potarazu was an ophthalmic surgeon in Maryland and holds degrees in business and medicine. He published Get Off the Dime: The Secret of Changing Who Pays for Your Health Care *(2009) and was a regular contributor to CNN and the* Washington Post. *He is currently serving a ten-year sentence in federal prison, where he is working as a GED tutor. Potarazu proposes a renewed focus on literacy among the incarcerated, including more concerted efforts to measure literacy among the incarcerated, tailored recommendations and curricula to help incarcerated individuals improve their literacy, and strategies to incorporate data about literacy among the incarcerated into recidivism reduction programs.*

Over the years there has been significant debate about ways to lower recidivism and crime rates. While a lot of attention has been given to analyzing socioeconomic factors to help explain why certain people commit crimes or return to jail, the role of literacy and learning has not received enough focus.

The screening for literacy skills in the criminal justice system needs to be more comprehensive and consistent. Furthermore, disorders that impede basic literacy, such as learning disabilities and dyslexia, need to be screened for and managed in prison. While evidence-based programs to reduce recidivism are essential for an inmate's successful reentry to society, they may be ineffective for someone who lacks basic skills in reading and math.[1] Only by aggressively attending to the issue of literacy in our prisons and communities can we protect the potential for success in other reforms.

While rudimentary programs exist for addressing basic education in prison, my experience as an inmate and teacher has convinced me that there is an enormous opportunity for advancing substantial changes to the existing system. Literacy, as defined by the National Center for Education Statistics, is "understanding, evaluating, using and engaging with written text to participate in society to achieve one's goals and to develop knowledge and potential."[2] According to current estimates, there are approximately two million inmates in U.S. prisons.[3] At least 70 percent of all incarcerated individuals can read only at the fourth-grade level or below.[4] In 2006, the *San Francisco Chronicle* reported that research has shown that equipping inmates with a solid education is one of the surest ways of reducing the rate at which they end up behind bars after being released from prison.[5] High school dropouts are 3.5 times more likely than graduates to be arrested, and dropouts are 63 percent more likely to be incarcerated than their peers.[6]

Every rule has an exception. I have a medical degree from George Washington University and an MBA from Johns Hopkins. I am a highly specialized ophthalmologist and a businessman with experience in health care data and analytics. Despite my education and experience, I landed in prison. Does education really matter? It turns out that a good education in itself does not prevent bad judgment. I learned that the hard way. However, prison has afforded me an unusual opportunity to look at the impact of education through a different lens, one that has completely changed my perspective on learning. The seventeen years I spent in training to become a neuro-ophthalmologist and businessman seem limited compared to what I have learned about education and literacy in the prison system.

While many types of jobs are available in the prison camp, the obvious choice for me seemed to be the position of a GED teacher. I thought, how hard can it possibly be to teach basic English, math, science, and social studies? It turns out that it can be quite hard. The dynamics of teaching inside a prison are very different from those of a normal school environment. As part of a sentence, courts may mandate that inmates without a high school diploma are required to attend classes that will prepare them to earn a GED. Inmates who don't attend class can be subject to losing good-time days as well as other disciplinary action.[7] As a result, the classroom can be filled with inmates who are motivated to use their time wisely as well as those who have no interest in learning and can sometimes be disruptive. While I was advised to ignore those inmates who were not interested, it soon became clear to me that there were complex reasons for their apathy and inattention. Some of them lacked basic reading and math skills. I knew this because some would approach me after class outside on the running track in the recreation yard and ask for help. To make matters worse, inmates understandably don't want others on the compound to know that they lack basic literacy skills for fear of how they will be perceived by their peers. This dynamic caught me by surprise. I have never been in an environment where someone has been afraid to tell anyone they cannot read, living in fear that another inmate may find out. How did this situation get so bad?

At the time of incarceration, inmates each undergo an initial intake that involves a cursory review of their educational background. Also part of the ongoing review is an assessment of an inmate's overall progress in prison, which evaluates disciplinary issues, participation in education programs, and employment. This assessment creates a "custody score" that is periodically evaluated over the period of incarceration. But literacy skills are not part of this ongoing assessment.[8]

In some prisons, a standardized test called the Test of Adult Basic Education is administered to establish an inmate's functional level of education.[9] These scores can then be used to identify specific skill areas in reading and math that require reinforcement. A significant number of inmates screened by this test may have skills only at the fourth-grade level or lower.[10] While many factors are considered in the placement of an inmate in a particular prison, literacy is not one of them. Ensuring inmates are placed in prisons with appropriate educational programs to meet their needs is simply not considered at the time of processing. During incarceration, many inmates lack the skills even to read their legal documents or fill out forms required in prison. Many prisons offer programs for drug rehabilitation, and a prerequisite is that an inmate be able to read at the eighth-grade level to qualify for the program. But this criteria is not necessarily applied consistently across the system, and as a result there may be inmates participating in these programs who lack the basic skills to read and write their required assignments. If the basic issue of improving literacy in prisons is not addressed, it will be extremely difficult for rehabilitative programs to have an impact in reducing recidivism. What good are programs if inmates cannot qualify or cannot do the assignments because they lack basic reading or math skills?

While some prison curriculums offer instruction at the pre-GED level, many inmates fear the stigma of being seen in one of these "remedial" classes. The ability to provide tutoring on a one-to-one basis would require significant manpower, which simply does not exist, unless other inmates volunteer. The materials and resources available to teach basic literacy are limited. Many books are outdated. Audio-based programs and other applications that would be readily available outside prison are few. What is the solution?

My experience and observations as a GED teacher in prison are the basis for new concepts and programs that I developed and started to implement with the support of the prison staff here at FCI Cumberland over the past year. The objective of the framework is to focus on improving the assessment and advancement of basic literacy skills necessary to sustain the futures of inmates post-incarceration, ultimately reducing recidivism rates. Several key pillars serve as the foundation for my thesis.

First, to reduce recidivism rates, a consistent, systematic approach to accurately measuring literacy skills is critical. According to the recommendations of the First Step Act, passed in 2018, which expands programming with the aim of reducing recidivism rates, participation in "evidence-based recidivism reduction programs" is a key determinant in facilitating an earlier release of low-risk inmates to home confinement.[11] An inmate's ability to participate in these programs will be largely dependent on their basic literacy skills. As a result, a more detailed quantitative assessment of literacy skills at the time of initial incarceration will be crucial to match inmates to the appropriate facilities, as well as to programs that offer necessary resources. The assessment must be standardized and consistently administered across the prison system. As part of the implementation of the First Step Act, data collection efforts are pivotal for an accurate assessment of programs' ability to reduce recidivism rates. While many variables are listed in the new law that the Bureau of Prisons must gather as part of the National Prisoner Statistics Program, the assessment of literacy levels is not part of the current directive.[12] Ensuring that literacy levels are accurately measured and reported will be essential to assess adequately the effectiveness of recidivism programs.

While the Test of Adult Basic Education provides for detailed analysis of various skill areas, these results are not enough. The next generation of standardized assessments should also be able to make specific recommendations for resources and curriculum that will be used to further develop those skills. Currently, the approach is random and the materials available to teach the basic skills are limited and inconsistent. Such types of recommendations already appear in the results of the individual GED test reports.

Second, once a specific curriculum is chosen, a private learning environment is necessary to help the inmate advance. Without discretion, any effort is likely to fail because of the social stigmas involved. Herein lies the opportunity to enhance current educational facilities in prisons with technology that can enable dynamic audio teaching. This will not only enable a private environment but also facilitate customizing lessons for students according to their needs. A significant limitation in prisons is the lack of access to current technology that we use in our daily lives. Without access to these tools, merely advancing education through written means and textbooks is insufficient. Inmates expecting to return to society to lead successful lives will need to be able to assimilate quickly to commonly used technology. When the ultimate goal is to reduce recidivism, it is prudent to provide inmates with every opportunity and resource needed to seamlessly function in the workplace and society.

Third, technology enhancements are also necessary for evaluating the amount of data being collected. One of the key lessons I learned in health care over the years is that data is the most valuable commodity available for driving change. The struggle, however, is the time, effort, expertise, and technology required to process data that can create meaningful insights. If the ultimate goal is to establish programs that will reduce recidivism and crime rates, then access to accurate, insightful data that cuts across domains is crucial.

The First Step Act's proposed risk assessment tool will generate massive amounts of data. Collecting this information for the National Prison Statistics database will spawn even more elements to include in future recidivism reduction programs. There should be, superimposed on this dataset, measures of literacy and other relevant demographic indices that can have a measurable impact on rates of recidivism. This data is the ultimate asset that will drive reform for the criminal justice system. Such a vast amount of data must be supported by a sophisticated, scalable technology platform. Without such a foundation, any effort to assess accurately recidivism rates and other measures will be fraught with inefficiency, errors, and eventually higher cost.

The development of a risk assessment tool that includes the measurement of literacy and actual educational programs will require a substantial investment. Hiring engineers and scientists with experience in developing big-data solutions is an important step, but it will be expensive. Unfortunately, there is no shortcut around this. You get what you pay for.

With the proper infrastructure, clean data, and algorithms, it can be possible to tailor programs more accurately for individual inmates. Today the risk assessments that are being done are limited in scope considering the data that is available. Literacy is not a measure often included in software programs presently in use for custody and security assessments. Furthermore, programmatic recommendations are typically made in light of the limited number of options available at any given prison. A more robust assessment tool that includes other key metrics, such as literacy, can create an accurate correlation to recidivism rates. Through improved algorithms and expansion of the curriculum in recidivism reduction programs, it will be possible to curate a program plan that is tailored to an inmate's needs.

The success of the program is only as good as the objective measures of success that are established up front. How will we know if improving literacy rates will actually have an impact on reducing recidivism rates? While none of the answers will come overnight, it is important to establish a goal and a set of standards that the prison system works toward and can measure. In the end, if we improve literacy rates, we should be able to see a measurable decline in recidivism and crime rates. Over time, these correlations can be very helpful in better predicting who is more predisposed for recidivism.

Improving literacy can have a dramatic impact in reforming the criminal justice system and the lives of millions of people incarcerated who desperately need a chance to survive and thrive once they are released. Every American should be able to read, write, and do basic math. As the most advanced society in the world, our commitment should be to ensure that every individual has these fundamental skills, no matter their background.

As we prepare inmates for reentry into society, improving literacy in many areas can have a significant impact in ensuring that a person can find a job, keep a job, and never come back to prison. While literacy is often focused on reading and math, other basic knowledge is also important. As part of the Life Skills Program that I started at Cumberland, we teach basic health literacy on topics such as health insurance, drug addiction, mental health issues, and managing chronic conditions. In addition to health literacy, we teach basic skills in money management and budgeting. The goal of the Life Skills Program is to provide "comprehensive literacy" to facilitate an inmate's reentry into society. In the end, such programs benefit not only the inmate but also the community. The hope is that by improving the literacy of current and former inmates, and by keeping citizens productive, we can one day prevent crimes from happening in the first place.

Although I am highly educated with advanced medical training, my experience in prison has deepened my understanding of education. I look at my time in prison as a "residency in literacy and learning." Nothing is more gratifying than providing an education to someone who desperately needs help, and to improve their lives and the futures of their families. Improving literacy will enable prisoners to reenter society successfully, and will ensure the safety and prosperity of our communities for generations to come.

17

The Age of Inequality:
Ending the Mass Incarceration of Our Youth

Chris Dankovich

Chris Dankovich is an artist, teacher, tutor, and chef who has been incarcerated since he was fifteen years old. In that time he has won writing awards from PEN America, PrisonWriters.com, and Vidahlia Press and Publishing House, and has been published by the Harvard Educational Review, The Periphery *magazine, and* Fence *magazine. He is a regular contributor to* MinutesBeforeSix *and* PrisonWriters.com. *He is currently incarcerated in Michigan. He proposes to remove the financial incentives for counties to charge and incarcerate kids as adults and to limit prosecutorial discretion in juvenile cases.*

"D***it!" I said as I frantically looked around for someone I knew, a familiar face. I was panicking a bit. I was sneaking out in the prison unit, breaking the disciplinary sanction I had been given for smoking. Everyone else around me was allowed to smoke because they were old enough, but I still wasn't. The area where the iron was, tethered to the cinder-block wall above a floor of cold, gray tile, was only about twenty feet from the officer's desk, where there was an officer most of the time, but not now. I was looking around, nervous about staying out of my room that was at the other end of the hallway, trying to avoid getting caught, surrounded by unfamiliar people, and keeping an eye on the officers' station. I hurriedly tried to figure out how to turn on the clothes iron, slapping it a few times when the light didn't come on. Someone saw me and walked over. He asked me if I needed help, and showed me how to use it, helping me get the wrinkles out of my nicest prison shirt. I thanked him and asked if he wanted anything for helping me, but he turned me down. I had never used an iron before, never worn ironed clothes growing up. I had to take the risk, and take the chance to learn, though, because my older cousins Nick and Jon were coming to see me. I grew up idolizing them, and at sixteen I still did. I needed to look my best.

Beginning in the 1990s, facilities and programs designed to incarcerate, treat, and rehabilitate juveniles underwent a wave of remodeling and closure, and private entities or small, county-run programs took over.[1] In Michigan, as in much of the country, county governments in charge of sentencing juvenile "delinquents" also bear the financial burden of keeping and treating them.[2] This creates a perverse incentive to charge more juveniles as adults, in order to place them under the state's jurisdiction and shift the costs away from the counties.

At the same time, the country as a whole experienced a

national spike in fear of "child superpredators," stereotyped as black gang members and drug addicts bent on terrorizing and threatening communities. This fear led to the passage of new laws calling for juveniles to be sentenced as adults for many crimes (including nonviolent ones).[3] These laws left the decision about how to charge juveniles in the hands of local prosecutors. Another law prevented children from returning to juvenile court if they were ever charged with an "adult" crime, even if they were found not guilty, thus paving the way for de facto discrimination, most often against juveniles of color.[4]

Between 1990 and 1999, the number of juveniles (or people who started their sentences as juveniles) being held in adult jails ballooned by 311 percent. States were extremely late to the game of removing children from incarceration among regular adult offenders, where they were at enormous risk of being sexually and physically victimized.[5]

Thumb Correctional Facility, where I started my prison sentence, is the adult prison where Michigan has housed many juveniles since 2005. Inmates under eighteen incarcerated there now inhabit a "Youthful Offender" unit,* which contains a total of approximately four hundred inmates. Four hundred inmates may seem like only a small percentage of the approximately forty thousand inmates in Michigan's prison system, but that number fails to take into account the inmates who turn eighteen daily and are transferred (often on their birthdays) to adult prisons, where they are not

---

* "Youthful Offender" is the label for those who are chronological juveniles but who were legally emancipated into adulthood by a prosecutor's designation and sentenced as adults.

accounted for or tracked any longer.[6] Hundreds of thousands of such "grown" juveniles reside in the adult system, though the exact number is virtually impossible to calculate.

Steve grew up across the road from my grandparents' home, in the only other house for a half-mile on the outskirts of a town with a population of one thousand. I had never met him before I first spoke to him on the prison bus from the intake center in Jackson to the Thumb Correctional Facility. We were assigned to the same cell. I started showing him pictures that people had sent me from the outside. He stopped me when I showed him a picture with his house in it, saying, "I know where that is!" Impossible . . . no one knows where that is. Somehow my first bunkie in prison and I had something in common!

We went on and on, talking about all sorts of things, until all of a sudden, screams rang out down the hallway, followed by calls for help and someone slamming our window's shutter so hard it swung back open. We looked out and saw what looked like a dead body on a stretcher, covered in blood, followed by a muscled young man, now in handcuffs, walking cocky, bloody, and smiling. The medical staff struggled to find a pulse before they finally found the faintest one. Still in our first hour in prison, Steve and I looked at each other. Steve was almost two years older than I was, much bigger, and I looked to him for a bit of reassurance. He looked to me for the same thing. I might have been smaller, but I had a twenty-five-year sentence and a murder charge. He was just a kid who got caught with a stolen car.

While those who advocate for "adult time for adult crimes" say it is the only way to safeguard against "superpredators," the vast majority of children sentenced as adults are actually individuals like Steve.[7] From 2003 to 2013, over twenty thousand children were given adult sentences in Michigan, over eleven thousand of them for nonviolent offenses.[8] Most of them had no prior criminal record. Whereas young age is supposed to be a mitigating factor, children often receive not shorter but *harsher* sentences than adults for the same crimes, given the same circumstances.

In prison, you can almost start to think of the people in the cell next to you as your neighbor. When I was seventeen, I had a neighbor named Kevin who had been locked up since he was thirteen years old for holding up a pizza place, brandishing a harmless toy as a pretend gun. He served eight years, getting denied parole for a year his first time because of his multiple suicide attempts while in prison. When I was twenty-two, my twenty-one-year-old neighbor John was at Thumb for a string of armed robberies, knocking off a few liquor stores and gas stations with a loaded 9-millimeter. He wrote me a few times after he was released upon completing his five-year minimum sentence.

As a group beset by a number of challenges—no education, mental illness, broken homes, a history of regular abuse, and no option to legally participate in much of society—juveniles are the backbone of our adult mass incarceration problem.[9] To change our system of mass incarceration in this country, we must look at the hundreds of thousands of individuals who need to be reexamined, dealt with in a specialized way, and rehabilitated. Patricia Caruso, former director of the Michigan Department of Corrections, said: "It's not really a political question. If your focus is on public safety and community safety, you have to look at what works. Incarcerating teenagers in the adult system is not making us safer."[10] We can change the way we deal with children who are at risk of entering the adult system. We must get rid of the financial incentives to charge juveniles as adults.

Counties have limited budgets, out of which they must financially support incarcerated youths charged as juveniles. If, on the other hand, these youths are charged as adults, they are completely taken off the hands of the county and out of the budget of the county government.[11] The burden of juvenile rehabilitation and incarceration must be passed up to the state and federal level, and the trend in reducing the per capita numbers within juvenile facilities must be reversed in order to provide space for those who otherwise would be sent to adult prison. Most juveniles, even those that commit more serious crimes, should never be considered for the adult system. Those that have committed a nonviolent crime *absolutely* should never be. One of the arguments against sentencing older teenagers to juvenile sentences is that, in most states, the maximum age at which they can be held at a juvenile facility is eighteen, or in some cases twenty-one, at which time they must be released. This does not leave much time to treat or incapacitate a teen who committed a crime at age sixteen or seventeen, so the decision is made to treat the teen as an adult in order to give them a slightly longer sentence. However, the majority of juveniles sentenced as adults are *not* sentenced to long periods of time.[12] Most are not murderers or rapists.

The automatic release of a juvenile at age eighteen (or twenty-one) in many cases is an impediment to reasonable sentences in juvenile facilities. But eighteen and twenty-one are merely arbitrary numbers. At twenty-one, individuals are already past legal adulthood. Juvenile systems should be able to hold those who come in as juveniles until older ages for crimes that are more serious, subject to judicial review. This also would reflect the vastly different needs that a twenty-five-year-old prisoner who came in at fourteen years old has from a twenty-five-year-old prisoner who came in at twenty-one years old. Having been incarcerated since I was fifteen, I am today a nearly thirty-year-old man who has earned a college degree but doesn't have any idea what a social security number is for, what taxes I'll have to pay someday or how to pay them, or how to operate a bank account or use a credit card. I am currently engaged to be married, but I have never been on a date. I have no idea how to drive. Past a youthful offender's eighteenth (or twenty-first) birthday, they are no longer treated any differently than a forty- or sixty-year-old inmate, given no separate opportunities, no different classes, no other consideration or rehabilitation. For those who come in as youths whom we plan to release, it makes no sense not to teach them the bare essentials, and it makes no sense to treat them the same as those who committed crimes as adults. By changing where they are incarcerated and how they are treated, long-serving juveniles could be rehabilitated, decreasing the risk of recidivism. This creates a safer society and is less expensive in the long-term.

There is another way to change how children move through incarceration that would not cost a single penny and would increase fairness, objectivity, and transparency: remove prosecutors' arbitrary discretion to emancipate juveniles and charge them as adults. Prosecutors could still seek to have a juvenile treated as an adult in the most serious of cases, but the decision rightfully belongs in the hands of judges and jurors.

When it comes to juveniles, their own decision-making abilities are questioned and limited in nearly every way because they are not considered responsible for themselves. When juveniles are charged with a crime, it is not enough to merely prove that they did it. If they are to be treated as adults, it needs to be argued and proven that they did so with adult culpability and capability. Prosecutors have an incentive to appear "tough" on criminals, including youthful ones, and currently they may arbitrarily choose to charge a juvenile in whatever way they feel like, without being subject to oversight or even questioning. The discretion regarding how to treat and sentence a child rightfully belongs with a judge and jury, who have the authority to determine every other aspect of a criminal case.

Put together, these reforms would significantly reduce the number of juveniles incarcerated as adults in any given year, and they would lead to a dramatic decrease in the overall prison population within a decade. It would be a perfect and proper reform to our criminal justice system that would create a new paradigm in a fundamental way. Changing the traditional approach to hundreds of thousands of juveniles by treating them according to their age would mean a long-term decrease in the national prison population. There are no changes that could more dramatically affect this country's criminal justice system, and make it more just. It is time for a change, and the change needs to start with those who serve the hardest time: the hundreds of thousands who are thrown in adult prisons as juveniles. Many people, including legislators, don't know about the mass incarceration of youth or the seriousness of the epidemic. It's time they found out.

18

Prisons as Nursing Homes: A Taxpayer Debacle

Charles Patrick Norman

At the University of South Florida, Charles Norman studied finance, writing, and romance languages. While incarcerated, he won a MENSA scholarship, which enabled him to continue his college education. He has taught computer classes and writing, and has worked as a counselor as well as at a boot camp for first offenders. Winner of a number of prizes in the Prison Writing Program's annual contest, including first place for memoir in 2008, Norman has also won awards from Prison Life *magazine and most recently from the Tampa Writers Alliance. His essay "Pearl Got Stabbed" appears in* Doing Time, *the PEN American Center prize anthology, and more of his work, as well as more information about him, appears on a website, www.freecharlienow.com, which is maintained for him by friends on the outside. He proposes transferring certain elderly individuals incarcerated for life to private care facilities that are equipped to meet their specific health care needs, rather than using taxpayer money to subject them to inadequate care in prisons.*

Seventy-two-year-old John Simison sat on the curb in front of the bank he'd robbed moments ago, lit his last cigarette, and waited for the police to arrive. Suffering from emphysema and a host of other ailments, he hacked and coughed as he tried to inhale the nicotine-laden smoke. He'd passed a note to the teller demanding money with no dye pack, put a wad of twenties in his pants pocket, and slowly walked out of the bank to sit on the curb. He was unarmed. Two minutes later, police placed handcuffs on a frail John Simison and pushed him into the back of the patrol car for his ride to jail.

Since he'd robbed a state-chartered bank, John Simison pled guilty before a county judge and, due to his long history of prior bank robberies going back over fifty years, was sentenced to life in prison. In John's case, life in prison meant about one year.

He first went to Union C.I., Florida's oldest, largest, and most dangerous prison, a.k.a. "The Rock," Raiford, or the state pen. I'd met John in jail, and marveled at his exploits when he'd been a younger, healthier professional bank robber who had daringly escaped from several jails and prisons from Pennsylvania, Ohio, and Michigan, to Florida. Now he was so sick that he could barely walk to the shower. For a cigarette and a cup of coffee, though, John would regale the younger cellmates until his bad lungs set him off on another coughing jag.

Twice John was hit on the head by a white supremacist and robbed of his wristwatch, his only possession of any value. He'd been found unconscious on the prison rec yard and taken to the U.C.I. hospital until he recovered. After his first hospitalization, his watch was located and returned to him. The day after his return to open population, the same prisoner hit him on the head again, stealing his watch a second time. The robber served thirty days in solitary. The wristwatch was not recovered.

With his poor health getting worse, John was assigned to the prison hospital at Lake Butler in North Florida. Despite being transported to an outside hospital for treatment by specialists, he never recovered. One year later, John Simison died and was buried in a pauper's grave on Gopher Ridge, the name prisoners bestowed on the state cemetery. The outside grounds crew dug the grave. Inmates at the auto tag plant made a small half-size aluminum tag with John's prison number stamped on it and attached to a wooden stake. No name. A minimum custody chapel clerk read a few Bible verses.

Rough estimates put John's last year in state custody at a minimum cost to Florida taxpayers of over $100,000. (The prison doesn't publicize actual health care costs.) John's fate was not a rare occurrence. Similar stories are repeated in Florida prisons every year as thousands of elderly male and female prisoners with little hope for release get older and sicker, waiting to die, at incredible taxpayer expense.

Although the Department of Corrections estimates that the average inmate's annual cost of incarceration is less than $25,000—a $2.4 billion budget divided by 96,000 incarcerated—thousands of sick and elderly prisoners cost Florida taxpayers $50,000, $100,000, even hundreds of thousands of dollars a year each in medical care.[1] One heart attack, a triple bypass performed by a cardiologist at an outside hospital, and follow-up care could cost the state a quarter million dollars or more. A special cancer clinic at Lake Butler is at capacity daily, and MRIs, CT scans, and PET scans are performed on site. The private health care corporation with the prison contract bills the state the same as Medicare payments for the expensive screenings. Cha-ching!

With the latest court orders forcing the corrections department to treat thousands more prisoners suffering from hepatitis C, medical bills in the hundreds of millions of dollars threaten to sink the vastly strained prison health care system. This is not just a Florida problem, but one that saps the medical budgets of prisons nationwide, running into billions of dollars for health care. In effect, the prisons are turning into nursing homes.

Is there a better way? Of course there is. It is a matter of the politicians and "experts" agreeing on bold initiatives that will release thousands of now-harmless old men and women languishing in prisons, waiting to die.

My friend, Samuel D., I will refer to as "Red Devil," his chain gang nickname, since he is still alive, barely. Red Devil came to prison in 1968, at age eighteen. Fifty years later, he is totally blind and barely functioning. An "impaired inmate assistant" tends him, walks him to the chow hall with Red Devil's hand on his shoulder, sets him down at a table, brings back two food trays, cuts up his food with a plastic spork, feeds him, dumps the trays, and walks him back to his cell.

What does it cost to keep this man in prison, with his myriad health problems and failing brain? What risk could he pose to society? Wouldn't it be more humane and economical to release Samuel to a nursing home, billing Medicare $4,000 a month for his care, rather than costing the taxpayers $100,000 or more a year to keep him in prison until he eventually dies?

William Alexander was one of the oldest Florida prisoners, at eighty-eight years old, when a local newspaper did a feature story on elderly prisoners who had aged into harmlessness. What threat to society could this decrepit old man and many more like him be? In his younger years, Bill had been a brilliant architect who had designed the original monorail at Busch Gardens in Tampa. At seventy-seven, he'd shot and killed his wife. Eleven years later, a reporter asked Bill's trial prosecutor why he opposed an eighty-eight-year-old man's release—how dangerous could he be? The prosecutor said that as long as Bill had the strength in his finger to pull a trigger, he was dangerous.

William Alexander eventually died in prison, at considerable cost to the state.

The prison system did find a way to shave off a few dollars in funeral expenses by forgoing the Gopher Ridge services and burials. Henceforth, the Starke Funeral Home's contract with the state called for unclaimed prisoners' bodies to be cremated and otherwise disposed of.

Most prisoners are not long-term residents. Recent news reports on Florida prisons stated that about 33,000 prisoners— one-third the population—were released back into society last year. Many did not stay out for long, but found themselves back behind the razor wire fences after re-offending or violating their terms of release, such as changing their addresses, not maintaining a job, or flunking drug tests. Many others have been imprisoned three, four, five times—as many as eleven times, for some incorrigible offenders—served a few years on each sentence, got out, came back inside, over and over again, until they caught a more serious charge that imprisoned them until they died. We call that "Life on the Installment Plan."

Bottom line—prison is a revolving door for thousands of "short-timers" who come and go for relatively brief periods of freedom. But is a slow death sentence for thousands more, many who came to prison as young offenders, but thanks to harsh mandatory sentences from the 1970s, 1980s, and 1990s, are doomed to vegetate in prison until they die, or until the draconian laws are changed.

The arbitrary way release decisions are made makes bad situations worse. The three parole commissioners in Florida are not encumbered with such legal restrictions. Amazingly, Florida law requires only one qualification to be a parole commissioner—you must be a Florida resident.[2] You don't need a college degree, special experience, or training to make life or death decisions for several thousand elderly prisoners still under the authority of the parole commission. Political connections help. Whereas every step of the trial process is tightly controlled, the parole commission can sentence thousands of prisoners under their authority to "slow death sentences."

The parole commissioners maintain authority over murder cases committed before the 1994 mandatory "life without parole" (LWOP) law went into effect, and all other felonies committed prior to the 1983 "abolition" of the parole commission. Over 4,300 elderly prisoners under the authority of the parole commissioners remain in prison, subject to the whim of commissioners.

When a prisoner has completed the twenty-five-year mandatory portion of his or her life sentence, becoming parole-eligible, but the commissioners invoke a parole release date fifty or one hundred years away, far beyond that person's life expectancy, they are de facto sentencing that person to death, with none of the safeguards required of every other branch of the judicial system.

What cost to the taxpayers are thousands of sick, elderly, dying prisoners, blind, paralyzed, often suffering from dementia, running up medical bills in the hundreds of millions of dollars, when they pose little or no risk to society?[3]

When prisons are turned into nursing homes housing thousands of critical care inmates, the taxpayers are footing bills better served by releasing a large percentage of those sick and dying prisoners to private facilities better capable of caring for them until they die, without the significant extra costs of caring for the elderly and infirm in the context of a prison.

Not all the elderly candidates for release need to be housed in nursing homes or other private facilities. Although many of these prisoners have outlived most of their family and have no outside support, there are possibly hundreds who still have family willing to take them in, saving the state additional thousands of dollars. Some even have jobs at their advanced ages. Don Jones was seventy-nine years old when he was finally released from prison on parole after almost thirty years and went to "Prisoners of Christ," a residential faith-based transition program in Jacksonville, Florida. He got a job as the oldest bag boy at a Public supermarket, where he diligently worked for three years, until he died in a car accident. At least he got that time for freedom.

Of course, a screening process must separate those who

pose little risk to society from those too dangerous to release, no matter their mental or physical condition. The parole commission already has a program, for medical parole release, but to qualify for that, the inmate must be terminally ill, facing imminent death. There's little logic in such releases, since the prisoners are usually hospitalized, in terrible pain, often unconscious, going from the prison hospital to a hospice for their final days.

Most prisoners applying for medical parole die before obtaining commission approval. Such a program does nothing to cut the hundreds of millions of dollars presently spent on medical and the related security costs of caring for the incarcerated elderly. It makes both moral sense and economic sense to release at least two thousand elderly prisoners back into society, saving $200 million or more each year.

As for me, at age twenty-eight, in 1978, I was arrested by Tampa police detectives for a murder I'd been cleared of by other detectives three years earlier. Long, sad story. I refused increasingly lenient plea bargains offered by the prosecutor, proclaimed my innocence, and demanded a jury trial.

How could they find me guilty, a jury of my peers? I believed the propaganda, that twelve citizens would come to a true verdict, see past the lies. I'd watched Perry Mason.

No physical or forensic evidence connected me to the crime scene. Fingerprints did not match. The only eyewitness, Albert McKinley, a thirty-eight-year-old church deacon and the only non-felon witness, who had spent over an hour with the shooter, stated positively that I WAS NOT the culprit, who was much shorter and thinner than either of us.

Convicted felons given immunity for their perjured testimony implicating me in their crimes? How could that be? The actual shooter bragged that his wealthy father had paid off crooked cops and prosecutors to gain him and his crime partner immunity from prosecution for first-degree murder in exchange for their false statements that "Charlie told me he shot someone."

Everyone knows only the guilty are given immunity. The innocent don't need it.

Cut to the chase—against the odds, a gullible compromise jury found me guilty of murder and recommended life with a minimum twenty-five years before becoming eligible for parole. The prosecutor was not happy. After he offered me a final plea deal while the jury was out deliberating—fifteen years, second degree murder, no minimum, no mandatory, no opposition to parole, I'd mocked him, refusing the deal, confident I would be found not guilty by the jury, after two long days of deliberations. It was a mistake. My cavalier attitude drew his lasting enmity, and his opposition to my release has continued for over forty-one years, although I have lived an exemplary life in prison.

Upon my arrest at age twenty-eight, I was in the best physical shape of my life, having been involved in taekwondo and kick boxing, swimming, tennis, and golf for several years. When I entered prison at the Reception and Medical Center (RMC) at Lake Butler, examinations and tests by prison doctors confirmed my excellent physical condition. Forty-one years later, at age seventy, my health is a far different matter.

In 2007, I took a long prison van ride from Tomoka C.I. in Daytona to the RMC prison hospital, accompanied by two costly security guards, to see an outside oncologist. Diagnosis: squamous cell carcinoma, a form of skin cancer. No big deal. The prisoner who accompanied me to RMC was diagnosed with melanoma, the same cancer that killed Bob Marley. My friend has been dead for years. The dermatologist burned off a dozen or more lesions on my forearms, cheek, and scalp, prescribing several months of chemotherapy. The skin cancer went into remission for ten years, but finally came back in 2017, resulting in more trips to RMC to see specialists and receive treatments.

I was shocked at what I saw upon my first trip to the RMC prison hospital. The narrow hallways were crowded and congested with dying old men in wheelchairs, slumped, most too weak and pallid to hold up their heads. My subsequent trips over the past twelve years since that first trip to RMC only confirmed what my eyes told me years before: old men are dying like flies, and nobody seems to care. Every time I go there, broken men I once knew as strong young men hail me, recognizing me when I don't recognize their wrecked visages, recounting their litanies of ailments, lung cancer, heart disease, COPD, brain tumor, you name it, every one worse than I am, closer to dying. I say prayers for them and myself, thanking God for so far sparing me the burdens my brothers bear.

For the first twenty years of my imprisonment, I'd go along with the prison estimate of incarceration costs at $25,000 a year for a total of $500,000. But the past twenty-one years of my incarceration have been complicated by cardiac and blood pressure issues; treatment for kidney stones at Jacksonville Memorial Hospital; increasing arthritis; vertebra narrowing affecting my spinal cord, complicated by falling backwards off a prison bus in the rain, legs shackled, in 2014; and a new, possibly incurable neurological disorder that requires more outside testing. I would estimate the cost at a minimum of $50,000 a year, or over $1,000,000.

Overall, I estimate it has cost the state of Florida more than $1.5 million to keep me in prison for forty-one years, and I am relatively healthy compared to thousands of others.

Multiply that $1.5 million by 1,000 aged people serving life sentences, and states are spending somewhere in the ballpark of $1.5 BILLION, per 1,000 prisoners.

How does releasing elderly prisoners actually save the taxpayers money? First, when we talk about the high costs of prison health care, into the hundreds of millions of dollars for thousands of patients, no one talks about price-gouging or corrupt billing practices that have little if any oversight. For instance, the prison medical departments distribute appointment lists for dozens of prisoners to see one doctor the following day. If a prisoner doesn't show up, he or she will receive a disciplinary report that could result in confinement. Dozens wait hours for a five-minute "consultation," and others are "rescheduled." But according to the corporation, the prison is billed full value for all of those appointments. There aren't enough hours in a day.

What about transferring the costs from the prison medical system to outside, private nursing homes? Where are the savings? In prison, prisoners cannot collect social security or military retirement, even though they may have been receiving such retirement or disability checks when they were free, "on the street." Many prisoners, if released, would qualify for Medicare, Medicaid, and VA benefits, which would cover nursing home and hospital care. Shifting the medical expenses from state taxpayers to federal programs that the elderly prisoners already qualify for, in conjunction with the basic savings of not confining these individuals, reduces the direct burden on taxpayers.

But there were no programs available for John Simison when he got out of prison the last time. The Salvation Army offered him and others like him a cot and soup kitchen food for forty-eight hours, then he was back on the street. The $50 handed him before he got on the Greyhound bus didn't last long. He had no choice. By robbing a bank, he automatically qualified for a prison nursing home bed.

Society must address this issue now. Our system has inadvertently turned prisons into nursing homes, and the only way to solve this growing problem systematically is to release the harmless elderly prisoners and assist them in getting the help they need outside the prison context. The current correctional emphasis on "short-timers," offering reentry classes in a vain attempt to stanch the flow of young criminals back into the prison system, ignores the sick, dying, elderly elephant in the room—thousands of prisoners breaking the back of the prison health care system.

Angered that the jury did not recommend death in my case, after I rejected his plea offers, the corrupt prosecutor who was forced to suborn perjury to obtain a wrongful conviction was overheard saying, "Norman will never survive a life sentence."

I've done my best to prove him wrong.

19

In Defense of Survival: Incentivizing Good Behavior

Shirley Anne McCulley

Shirley Anne McCulley is currently incarcerated in Georgia, serving a life sentence for murder since 1997. She enjoys creating things in many forms and plans to work with her hands by retrofitting Airstream trailers upon her release. She proposes the creation of an incentive program to reward people for good behavior and improve their lives in prison.

In 1997 I was convicted of murdering my ex-boyfriend and am therefore labeled a violent offender. Before this tragedy, I had no personal experience with our criminal justice system. Before this tragedy, I had the luxury of thinking our jails and prisons were full of bad people who deserved to suffer and be punished for their misdeeds. Before this tragedy, I was naïve, judgmental, and often wrong about criminal justice.

Over the twenty-one years of my incarceration I've identified dozens of systemic problems for which I could not imagine a comprehensive solution. After feeling extreme frustration with the fact that, no matter what I do right, I found myself always in the exact same situation as women who are generally disruptive, and who spit on other inmates and even cut and stab them, I thought of a possible solution for my particular problem.

Before I get to my suggestion, I'd like to detour with a discussion of the label "offender." If the Georgia Department of Corrections wants better behavior out of its charges, it should cease labeling us as offenders, since the label really means "those who cause displeasure."[1] Instead, I will refer to myself and others as "inmates" throughout this piece.

Humans, for the most part, will repeat behaviors for which they are rewarded (or that are intrinsically rewarding) and cease behaviors that incur costs. Let's face it, most of the prison population has a behavior problem and is not inclined to follow rules. Yet in my admittedly limited experience, prison rewards bad behavior and ignores good behavior, thereby missing a simple and easy opportunity for retraining inmates to follow the rules.

If you have never been to prison, you might wonder, "How is bad behavior rewarded?" If you have been to prison, it is likely that several examples have already come to mind. Allow me to attempt an explanation.

The most obvious reward is intrinsic to the behavior—think wearing contraband, altered, or free-world clothing is rewarding because it is more comfortable, colorful, and attractive. Certain problem inmates achieve more substantial awards through cultivating familiarity with the correctional staff. And when those inmates ask, or demand, to speak with whoever is in charge, they usually get to speak to those authorities. They are not dismissed out of hand anywhere nearly as often as the rest of us. When a special detail comes up, or the parole board calls with a request for recommendations, it is these problem inmates, those who cause the most trouble, who come to mind and get those perks and recommendations. These are the largest and most obvious rewards that are essentially doled out for bad behavior.

Most inmates exhibit minor behavioral problems rather than huge ones. By ignoring tolerable and good behavior, the DOC actually encourages *more* bad behavior. Here are two specific examples:

Four women recently cut other women with broken-down razors. As punishment, our entire compound of over 1,700 women was put on razor restriction for thirty days—0.23 percent of our population was behaving extremely badly, yet the remaining 99.77 percent was forced to sacrifice personal hygiene for thirty days, through no fault of our own.

A more common injustice happens at count time: an officer steps into our dorm, tells us either to go to our rooms for count or to lock down for count, and then they leave. Most of us follow orders and go to our rooms. About 10 percent, always the same people, stay in the day area as if they heard nothing. When the officer comes back, they may let the infraction slide, or they may lock the whole dorm down for another hour, or more. What never occurs is the simple, targeted punishment of the individuals who disobey orders.

What this means to me, the inmate, is that regularly following rules and instructions actually "costs" me. I cannot shave, and I am stuck in my room for the misbehavior of others. My hair is thinning from constantly being pulled tightly back and up since female inmates are required to keep hair off of our faces and collars. More setbacks of this nature impede my experience here. While I am never going to start acting out or causing others grief, I have stopped following some of the rules I find inconvenient. Following them gets me nowhere, and often I get just as severely punished as if I hadn't personally broken the rules.

I propose the DOC implement a Raising Inmates Social Elevation (RISE) program. The purpose of RISE is to incentivize and reward good behavior, in order to encourage more good behavior and raise morale among inmates.

RISE would operate on a system of points that would accumulate over the course of an inmate's incarceration beginning on day one. One point would be gained for 365 consecutive days an inmate has not had a formal sanction on his or her behavior (in Georgia, this sanction is known as a Disciplinary Report, or DR). When an inmate receives a DR, if he or she is found guilty the day after that DR is written, a new countdown begins.[2]

Georgia's Department of Corrections also has less punitive sanctions in the form of verbal warnings and DR warnings.[3] Instead of a full RISE profile point, a verbal warning could deduct 0.1 of one (worth about thirty-six days) with no disruption to the actual day count. A DR warning would subtract 0.2 of a point (worth about seventy-two days) with no disruption to the actual day count. Nobody's RISE profile would ever drop below zero; this is not meant to be a punitive program.

RISE profile points would be displayed on inmates' schedules, printed every three months. Inmates would have to carry their schedules at all times. These would have a section for medical profiles, which would be an ideal place to insert RISE profile points and thus make it easy for staff to identify an inmate's level of privilege. Initial implementation might prove to be a little confusing, especially for those who have been incarcerated for a long time. But for incoming inmates, opening and maintaining RISE profiles would be very simple.

I have come up with a sample list of actual incentives that the DOC could reasonably allow. Any new property items could be introduced as RISE profile perks.

1 point—May participate in special compound activities, such as talent shows.

2 points—May have prescription or reading glasses sent from home.

3 points—May have kindergarten scissors, 100 percent plastic.

4 points—May have photos decorating locker exterior.

5 points—May have UVA/UVB protection sunglasses.

6 points—May have their package limits increased to $125 or 18.75 lbs., up from $100 or 15 lbs.

7 points—May have one board game sent from home.

8 points—May wear hair down.

9 points—May wear tennis shoes anytime.

10 points—May make 1 comfort move per year if someone is willing to swap.

11 points—May have 15 people, up from 12, on visitation list.

12 points—Monthly popcorn and movie day.

13 points—Quarterly personals bag.

14 points—May organize your locker your way.

15 points—Package ordered through retailers.

Prison staff members are already overburdened, so facilities would need to create the position of a RISE coordinator to assist wardens, families, and inmates in making the RISE program a success. The following are my recommendations regarding that position:

- In Georgia, the RISE coordinator would not require additional funding. Instead, similar to how commissary personnel are currently compensated, the RISE coordinator would be paid with inmate funds.
- Each prison should have at least one RISE coordinator and at least one position that can be held by volunteers. As a cost-saving measure, smaller facilities can share a coordinator, who would have an office at each of those facilities.
- RISE coordinators should maintain a page online as a resource for inmates' loved ones, with coordinator contact information, answers to frequently asked questions, and full details about the process of ordering and shipping products to inmates.
- RISE coordinators should liaise between inmates and their loved ones, scheduling and holding meetings with inmates regarding their RISE profile points, product choices, and family points of contact to answer questions and clarify policies. Coordinators should assist family members of inmates with the ordering process, even placing orders themselves once payment is received.
- RISE coordinators must be familiar with all restrictions to property to ensure that family members do not inadvertently purchase an item that security regulations will not allow their loved ones to receive.

Our society has long had the perception that inmates are bad people who deserve bad living conditions. That perception is evolving. Taxpayer dollars are now being spent on new rehabilitative programs. Policies are now focused on being "smart on crime" rather than the "tough on crime" approach that has proven ineffective.[4] RISE would begin the rehabilitative efforts as soon as an inmate arrives. The program would cost taxpayers absolutely nothing. It would involve small privileges and makes inmates accountable for those privileges. RISE would increase inmate morale and the inclination to cooperate with authority. This will make for a less stressful, and ultimately safer, environment for inmates and for staff.

Of course, RISE will not solve all discipline problems, but it would be a large step in the right direction. It would include 100 percent of the inmate population, would remain consistent throughout the prison sentence, and would be free to the taxpayer. RISE is the perfect example of being "smart on crime."

20

Electoral Politics: The New Revolution

Lewis Conway Jr.

Lewis Conway Jr. has almost two decades of experience in the broad-cast and music industry. He spent 2,095 days in Texas prisons and 4,012 days on parole for voluntary manslaughter. He was the first formerly incarcerated person in Texas to have his name on an electoral ballot when he ran for Austin City Council. On November 6, 2018, he garnered 11 percent of the vote, ultimately losing his first bid for political office. Conway is currently a campaign strategist with the ACLU. His proposal is to inform formerly incarcerated people about careers in public service, including running for elected office.

The value of civic engagement is self-evident. Research has demonstrated a connection between voting and desistance from crime. In other words, enfranchisement could lower recidivism and crime rates in general.[1] This correlation became particularly clear to me when I, a person with a conviction, ran for office in the state of Texas. When I stood on the front steps of the Austin City Hall, having just filed to be on the ballot for the 2018 elections, I never imagined the tsunami of events that would ensue. My campaign speech included the following words:

> You see folks like me aren't supposed [to] run for office. Running for office was not part of my parole plan. Can you imagine if it was? Can you imagine what my trajectory would have looked like? Well, today we run into the history books. Today the People make history in Austin, Texas. Today, Austin embraces change. Today, Austin becomes truly a Fair Chance city. Today, we take the first steps towards becoming a more compassionate, inclusive and equitable city. A radical city. Not reckless with wanton abandon, but radical because we are willing to pursue change. Radical means to us that we are willing to pursue and implement change.[2]

The campaign events would culminate on May 22, 2019, when the Texas attorney general released an opinion against my campaign and the Austin city attorneys' position in support of my interpretation of the election code.[3]

For fifteen years after my release, I had sought nothing more than to be a normal, taxpaying citizen and return to my community, quietly getting about the business of being a human again. Were it not for the scarlet letter of conviction that I carry, all of that would have been possible. From lacking a job that paid a living wage to lacking shelter for my family, I have been denied access to basic amenities and the means for self-sufficiency because of my past. The consequences that I continue to face because of that barred access include disabilities, lack of health care, homelessness, and at times even suicidal feelings.

Eight of the first seventeen black U.S. congressmen were born as slaves. They served at the beginning of the Reconstruction era.[4] Some of these men barely three years removed from slavery were serving as U.S. congressmen, fighting for and implementing policy. These men, whose labor once buttressed the sole source of economic wealth in the South, now wrote policy that would dismantle that same insidious market of buying and selling flesh. Because they had been born in those conditions, they were perfectly situated to rehabilitate the country from its corrosion during slavery. Their understanding of how to address the issues of slavery was born of their experience, a deeper knowledge they may have never achieved were it not for their tragic origins.

But the promise of Reconstruction, as illustrated by the new leadership of black U.S. politicians, was not fulfilled. The Southern planter class led the undoing of Reconstruction and then, over the course of the next century, managed to root their evil in state constitutions, including here in Texas.

At the root of incarceration is policy, much the same as it was with slavery. And because that same evil still grips our state and federal law, we must pull policy in our direction. We, people with conviction histories, need to be the ones writing policies if we want them to positively affect us. It won't come naturally, and it only starts by understanding the core problems. Only when we determine the why, how, and who behind the proverbial pothole in the middle of the street can we begin the work of decarcerating local jails and state and federal prisons. Only when those of us who are most affected by criminal justice policy are the ones directing that policy and stewarding those resources will we see anything that looks like abolition in our lifetime, our children's, or their children's.

We are in what I call the New Revolution, and I want the people most directly affected by prisons to be known as the new revolutionaries. Folks like me aren't supposed to engage politically; that's evident in how long it took formerly incarcerated folks to get the right to vote. However, it's folks like me who should frame the conversation when we talk about electoral politics. Folks most directly affected by the policies that govern their lives are the vanguard of electoral politics, because we seek systemic, radical, and transformational change: change that results in working families and poor people realizing the best quality of life possible, and that makes arrests and incarceration the final option rather than the first.

On my last day of incarceration, I sat in a humid and suffocating gymnasium along with seventy-five other men, waiting for our release. The place was packed, and the tension in the air was thick with anticipation and trepidation. As I scanned the faces around me, my eyes landed on a familiar face. He nodded his head at me in recognition and waved me over. We chatted about the units we had been on and where we had met. As he spoke, it dawned on me—he had been released and reentered more than once. I don't remember much about the rest of our conversation, because I was still trying to wrap my mind around his recidivism. During the early part of my incarceration when I was toiling in the "fields" picking fruits and vegetables, I had decided that coming back to prison was not an option for me.

I began to panic as he spoke and I wasn't sure why. With every word he spoke about how he had gone home and come back to prison, made parole, caught another charge, got convicted, and was now paroling again, I grew more flabbergasted. I couldn't imagine coming back to prison after all the days and letters I wrote home about not ever wanting to be incarcerated again.

One thing that drove the brother I was speaking to back to prison was his refusal to get out of the streets—or so I thought. He didn't talk about working and living a life that would keep him out of prison, so I figured I had the key to avoiding his fate: a job. If I could just get a job, then everything would work itself out. I could get an apartment, maybe even meet the pen pal I had been writing to and take her on a date. I didn't want to be too picky, so once I was released I shot as low as I could: McDonald's. I thought that if I could get a job at McDonald's, then everything would work out. Just like Eddie Murphy in *Coming to America*, I would move from the fryer to the grill and finally become a manager. I could even list the eight years of experience I had in the prison food service department in my application. My plan was perfect, until it wasn't.

I want to interject a thought here: What if I hadn't shot as low as I could? What if running for office had been part of my plan of action at the beginning? What if, when envisioning my life outside of prison, I had considered being a community

organizer, or maybe even a criminal justice organizer, working for a nonprofit to organize people directly affected by the
criminal justice system? The problem is that I didn't know
that was possible. My background didn't have to be a stum-
bling block; it could actually be a springboard.

At no juncture was I introduced to community organizing
while on parole. Granted, criminal justice reform wasn't as
big as it is now, but some of my colleagues were involved all
across the country back then, so conceivably I could have got-
ten involved as well. My parole officer made it clear that helping me find employment was not part of his job description,
but sending me back to prison if I didn't find a job *was* under
his purview.

When I first showed up at McDonald's after eight years of
incarceration, never having applied to a "real" job before, I
was eager, if somewhat apprehensive. When I was given the
application, however, right below my name, in the first set of
boxes the question froze me then, and would later freeze my
life. The question asked about my criminal history and gave
me a two-by-two-inch box to describe what happened. I was
paralyzed. How do I explain the last eight years of my life,
and the incident that led up to it, in a two-by-two box?

In the smallest handwriting I could manage, in as few
details as possible, I wrote about why I had gone to prison.
After completing the application, I felt relieved because I had
told the truth, and, knowing how important it was to tell the
truth, I thought, *of course* I would be rewarded. When the
manager read over my application, he paused and looked up
at me, went back to reading, and nodded his head. He placed
the application down and without blinking said, "Give

us a couple of days to look over your application and we'll call you."

Twenty years since, I haven't received that call, nor any calls from the hundreds, truly hundreds, of applications I sent out over the years. My saving grace was growing up with a father who was an entrepreneur after he retired from working with the Texas Comptroller's Office. Over the next twelve years I spent on parole, I was able to build businesses, and those businesses allowed me to stay out of prison. However, often those businesses were reliant on customers who were experiencing a downturn in their respective industries. At times I was working as a strip club DJ, music video producer, and cooking show host just to stay employed and out of prison.

Electoral politics became a source of possible employment when I got involved in the successful campaign to pass the only Fair Chance Hiring Ordinance in the South.[5] That effort was led by formerly incarcerated people who were directly impacted by unfair and discriminatory hiring practices. When the ordinance met immediate resistance at the state level, we were forced into legislative politics.[6] Natural lobbyists that we were, we led with our hearts, took on seventy-six conservatives, and won.[7] That victory is what prompted people to ask me to run for office. It just so happened that I was unemployed during most of that process because of my background.

When I canvassed the same neighborhood I used to sell crack in to register people to vote, I was met with the reality that I was evolving from organizer to politician. It met me on the doorstep of an elderly woman I'll call Ms. Sally. I knocked on her door and asked her whether she was registered to vote, and she said she was. I then asked her how she felt about criminal justice reform and immigration rights. She said, "Son, I care about that pothole out front my house there. Every time I back out, my back tire dips in that hole and makes my car shake. That makes my back hurt and I can't afford to go to the doctor no more until next year. Understand?"

I realized that she was living in a neighborhood that had been historically a drug haven and was being overtaken by gentrification. All she cared about was the pothole in front of her house and my plan to fix it. I became energized, because finally I had been presented with an opportunity to connect prisons to potholes—to electoral politics.

Eventually I was elected the political director for the Austin chapter of the Second Chance Democrats, a political club started by another formerly incarcerated political advocate. If a pathway into electoral politics could do this for my life, imagine what it can do for the seventy million other Americans that share my background?[8] It is imperative to think not only of the present but of future generations, and to consider what we need for our country at the local and national level. We need to shoot higher, and to do that, we have to push past where we need to be to land where we actually *want* to be.

21

Wards of the State

Arthur Longworth

Arthur Longworth is a contributing writer with The Marshall Project, a 2018 Pushcart Prize nominee, a six-time PEN America Prison Writing Award winner, and a 2019–2020 PEN America Writing for Justice Fellow. He has written for Medium, VICE News, *and* Yes! *magazine. His work has been presented onstage by renowned literary figures Francine Prose, Junot Diaz, and rapper/poet Talib Kweli. He is the author of* Zek: An American Prison Story *(Gabalfa Press, 2016). Arthur grew up in the foster care system. That is to say, Washington State raised him in its archipelago of infamous boys' homes, including one the* Seattle Times *dubbed a "house of horrors." The state turned him out onto the streets at sixteen years old without an education, job training, or money. He has a life without parole sentence and has been incarcerated for thirty-five years. Arthur proposes the creation of a "Youth Advocates" program to monitor and support foster youth throughout their trajectories in the criminal justice system.*

The juvy sits atop a broad swathe of sloping lawn, which is probably why the facility was called Hillcrest when it opened in 1948. A year later, however, when a seventy-two-year-old judge who was better known for fishing than for judging died while still in office, county officials renamed the site after him. Aside from a few historic vagaries, though, this juvy isn't different than any other juvenile detention center: it's used to administer incarceration. If you're uncertain or unaware of what that process is or how it works, let me run it down for you.

If you have a family, then you likely did more than run away, steal from a store, or get into a fight at school. These are offenses for which the cops, store owners, and school officials generally won't have you locked up. Rather, the inclination is to hand you over to your family. So, chances are, you fucked up worse than that and earned the trip to where you now stand handcuffed in front of this counter. But you still don't have much reason to worry. For nearly anything you could have done, the judge will release you to the "recognizance" of your family. You'll get to await your court date at home. And even if you are eventually sentenced to a stint locked up, I imagine incarceration will work in the way it was intended. That is, you'll be ashamed of your arrest and incarceration, you'll be frightened by the experience, and when you're released into the waiting embrace of your family, you'll feel obliged to do better. To be fair, there may be more to this experience than I'm relating. I cannot be sure, because it's never been my experience.

If you're a ward of the state, on the other hand, I can describe exactly what your experience will be. Lacking the options available for a young person who belongs to a family, you'll be taken to the juvy for running away from state placements that you feel are unlivable—for shoplifting or other petty crime you commit while trying to survive on the streets—or for getting into a fight or other trouble at a school that doesn't want you there anyway. When you land handcuffed in front of that counter, you are home.[1] That is, you *won't* be released on "recognizance" to await a court date. And incarceration won't work on you the way it works on others. You aren't ashamed of your arrest—because you have no one to be ashamed before, and you feel like whatever you did was in the interest of survival anyway. You find that being locked away is no scarier than the circumstance you came from—in fact, it's less so. And although you can't know what situation you'll be delivered into if you make it out of there, you have every reason to believe it'll be worse than what you faced before you entered. So incarceration, for you, doesn't feel like an experience you could have avoided—it feels inevitable.

A pair of staff in latex gloves usher you down a windowless corridor and into a bare holding cell. They press into the constricted space with you, which feels too close. And the crowded feeling is exacerbated when they remove the handcuffs and order you to "strip."

There isn't any way past them—no gap between or around them through which you can launch yourself and make it out of the cell. You know because, instinctively, you look for it. Even if you were to make it past them—which you won't—there isn't anywhere for you to go.

At this point, if you have a family and no prior experience

of the state or incarceration, you balk. That is, you find you're incapable, at least at that moment, of movement or the ability to carry out what the staff has ordered you to do. Something inherent to the experience of having parents prevents you from proceeding. Perhaps it's something your parents have inculcated in you as far back as you can remember, or that the privilege of their home has kept you, until now, from ever being ordered to disrobe in front of people you don't know.

Whatever your issue, you have to get over it. That is, they won't jump on you immediately—but they are unyielding. They make it clear to you that you will not leave the cell, and they will not back off, until you do what they tell you. And, one way or another, you will—I promise you.

If you're a ward of the state, on the other hand, you come into the situation already knowing that the staff—or any other state actor—won't exercise the same level of patience with you as they will with a young person from a family. You're also unburdened by whatever moral obstacle it is that a family imparts. Which means, when the staff order you to strip, you hide and suppress your discomfort, you get your back as close to the rear of the cell as possible, and you take off your clothes.

The air is unmoving and laden with the smell of dirty socks. You imagine it's the agglomerated funk of everyone who's stripped in that space before you. When you get your socks off, you feel the grit on the filthy concrete beneath your feet.

The staff take everything from you as you remove it and hand it over. They search each item and drop it into a brown paper bag. Shoes first. Everything else on top of them.

They order you through the obligatory "squat and cough"

contortions of the strip search which, weirdly, centers staff attention on your balls and butt. This is where you, as a ward of the state, hold an advantage over anyone privileged with a family. Because the demeaning nature of the search ain't really nothing compared to the ways you've already been demeaned before you arrived there. The cognitive and emotional calluses you had to develop in relation to humiliating experiences enable you to get through the process without wavering or allowing any expression, other than disdain, to show on your face

One of the staff steps out of the cell. He returns a moment later and hands you underwear that's been worn by innumerable others, a two-piece uniform with no pockets, and a worn pair of plastic slippers. As you put on the institutional clothing, you note that the namesake of the juvy (the long-dead judge) is stamped on every item. Staff members give you a bedroll and towel. You drape the towel around your neck and follow them out of the cell.

You continue down the corridor. The inability to extricate yourself from this place or circumstance, along with the movement deeper into the facility, evokes within you an escalating sense of being swallowed. Your mind conjures the image of a Beast down whose gullet you are passing. A hulking steel gate slides open as you approach and the staff steer you through it into the Beast's belly.

The staff members direct you across the vaulted expanse that separates the control center and the entrance of each hall. You pass a rollaway basketball hoop and a television situated on a ledge high on a wall. With the staff, you proceed to the hall you were assigned by the control center.

The only hall they won't take you to is the one farthest to the right because that's where they keep the girls. Girls are only in one hall because there are always fewer of them in this place than boys. You don't often see them, save for a potential glimpse in the probation department, or sometimes when you're en route to or from court.

If you have a family, you may not even know a girl who's been incarcerated.

If you're a ward of the state, on the other hand, nearly every girl you know has been locked up. Which, of course, is because state girls ain't got it any better than you. In fact, they often have it worse.[2] When your caseworker moves you to a bad state placement, ain't no one can make you stay: you run when you see that it's unlivable, or just whenever you see fit. But girls don't always have that choice. And when you're on the streets, you don't have to worry about as many things as they do. So, even though the Beast swallows fewer girls than boys, that's of little solace to you because it swallows the girls you're closest to. It swallowed my sister when she was nine.

It's four and a half steps to the rear of the cell and four and a half steps back to the door. You don't know when you enter the cell precisely how many steps and partial steps it takes to pace the length of the constricted space, or at which spot and in which direction you'll turn around. It's a learning process. One you learn so well that you awaken at night dreaming you're still pacing the cell.

A narrow bunk fabricated of steel plate is bolted to the concrete wall. And a mattress—which is really just a plastic cover over a thin foam pad—lies folded in half on the bunk. There's no pillow.

You make the bunk, if you're so inclined. Which means, if you have a family, you do your best to make the bunk like your bed at home. You unroll the bedroll and knot the corners of the sheet around the mattress pad, then lay the pad flat on the steel plate. When a staff face appears in the frame of unbreakable glass in the cell door, you ask about a pillow because you can't fathom a circumstance in which one would not be issued.

If you're a state kid, however, you don't ask for a pillow. You know you won't get one. And you don't want to provide anyone with the opportunity to laugh at you, or give them the satisfaction of telling you "no." You're accustomed to fending for yourself, so you don't actually even need the bunk, let alone a pillow. Outside the Beast, you know neither a regular home nor bed. Which means, you could as easily sleep on the floor as the bunk—it's all the same to you. You fold one of the blankets into as tight a bundle as you're able and wrap it in the sheet for a makeshift pillow. The rest of the bedding goes wherever.

You turn to the cell door. If it's your first time locked up and you're a ward of the state, you're likely young enough that you have to roll up your mattress and stand on it to see out the door. I did.

The door opens outward. The door's outer face—the side facing into the hall—is unmarred. However, its inner face—the side that's in the cell—hosts a melee of names and sentiments scratched into it from top to bottom.

If you have a family, you probably don't know any names on the door. And despite the inherent impulsivity of your young mind, you don't feel the slightest compulsion to add yours to the mayhem. You know your name doesn't belong there.

If you're a ward of the state, on the other hand, you likely know more than one of the names on the door. And you scratch your name somewhere in the muddle because you feel that's exactly where it belongs.

The staff issue you a change of underwear and escort you to a shower at the head of the hall three times a week. And you get an opportunity to exchange the uniform once a week. The day of the week the exchange takes place depends on which hall you're in.

There's a visiting process, so your family can come see you. If you're a state kid, however, that doesn't mean anything because you don't get visits. No matter how many times the Beast devours you, or how much more time you've spent in its belly than others, you're incapable of recounting for anyone what it's like to go to a visit. Because you don't know. All you know is the sound of the staff tapping a key on the doors of others in the hall to announce to them that they have a visit. You watch them pass your cell—the staff and the young person who has a visit—en route to a part of the facility you haven't seen, because it's not for you. Sometime later, they return. That's all you know.

You learn to "sign." That is, the boy in the cell across the hall, with patience and persistence, teaches you the hand formulations of the alphabet and gesticulations of unspoken language. To the best of your ability, you spell out words, aggregate them into sentences and compose entire conversations. When staff come for the boy across the hall and take him away, it's your job to teach the next boy they put in the cell.

Signing is prohibited, of course. But staff can't stop what they don't see.

The language becomes second nature to you. If you're a state kid, you sometimes use it in the boys' homes you're sent to between stints inside the Beast. And you're still fluent when you return. Like the strip search procedure, you don't forget how to do it.

There's a process for mail. Staff pass by your cell with mail they slide beneath the door of whichever kid it's addressed to. At night, just before the final shift change of the day, staff pick up letters that kids push out from beneath the doors for mailing. If you're a ward of the state, however, you don't have to worry about staff slipping a letter under your door. Nor do you slide any out.

At meal times, staff open the hatch in the door and hand a plastic tray through the opening. There isn't enough food on the tray, so you eat everything. If you're a state kid, you lick the tray. When staff return and again open the hatch, you push the tray out hoping they don't notice. When they laugh or comment about how clean the tray is, you feel shame. And, conversely, you feel gratitude toward the staff who simply throw the tray on the cart, slam the hatch, and move on.

The last tray of the day comes in the late afternoon. And in the interminable stretch of time between when you finish the tray and when the next tray comes at 7 a.m., your stomach collapses in on itself and locks into a fist. If you're a ward of the state, you already know this empty feeling well. Although familiarity doesn't make it any easier.

At no time inside the Beast do you contemplate the effect the experience has on you. You can't because you're in the midst of it. You're focused on trying to get through and make it out the other side. If you have a family and community, you may never have to think deeply about this experience. You don't have to, because when you get out, your family and community has you. You can forget and move forward. If you're a ward of the state, on the other hand, you WILL think about the experience, and re-live it unceasingly, when you get to prison. I promise you.

Juvenile and adult criminal justice systems presume—or work best in conjunction with—family and community support. Consequently, these systems impact foster youth, who lack such support networks outside incarceration, differently than they impact non-foster youth. As a consequence, foster youth are disproportionately represented in juvenile and adult criminal justice systems across the country and often find themselves locked in an institutional trap of recidivism or lifelong incarceration.

Family and community support facilitates successful transition through the criminal justice system. That is, support during incarceration, support upon release, and support through ancillary facets of the criminal justice system.

Support during incarceration includes visits, written correspondence, phone calls, appearance and advocacy at court hearings. This support motivates and empowers youth to avail themselves of opportunities to change their lives and to envision constructive paths forward after their release. Foster youth often lack these motivating and insulating forces in their lives.

Support upon release means being released from incarceration into the welcoming arms of a family and community. This support enables youth to actuate whatever plan they have made for a future. Foster youth, on the other hand, are too often released into the same, if not worse, circumstance that landed them in trouble in the first place.

Support through ancillary facets of the criminal justice system includes probation/community supervision, community service, and restitution/fines/court costs. This support enables youth to successfully negotiate and complete their legal obligations. Without this support, foster youth generally fail and return to incarceration.

In order to address this systemic failure, professional "Youth Advocates" administered by an independent nonprofit should follow foster youth under the age of twenty-five into, through, and out of juvenile and adult criminal justice systems to provide them with the support they inherently lack. The Youth Advocates' principal objectives would be: to support foster youths' successful navigation through, transition out of, and future diversion from the criminal justice system—to support foster youth in achieving the highest level of education/career preparation possible—and to support foster youth in developing, maintaining, and expanding family and community ties, which includes facilitating communication between incarcerated parents and their children.

Youth Advocates would carry out their objectives by providing foster youth a reliable, supportive, anchoring presence outside the institution within which they would otherwise be isolated. This external presence is key to motivating and empowering youth to avail themselves of the opportunity to change their life and to envision a constructive path forward after their release. Youth Advocates would help youth to develop and actuate their education, life, and career plan, beginning during detention, and would then connect them with the necessary resources upon release. Youth Advocates would meet with youth at least weekly, tracking their education and goal progress and providing or connecting youth to needed supports. Youth Advocates would be a part of the youths' case team, keeping in regular communication with their caseworker, foster parent, relative caregiver or group home staff, school administrators, counselors and teachers, and the court as needed. Youth Advocates would assist youth to successfully negotiate and complete their legal obligations. And, concomitantly, Youth Advocates would inform the court and request an alternate obligation when an imposed sanction is an impediment to a foster youth's success.

The Youth Advocate model would improve outcomes for incarcerated foster youth by increasing their level of education and career preparation—by helping them develop, maintain, and expand family and community ties—and by greatly reducing the recidivism rate of foster youth, as well as the child-welfare placement and incarceration rate of their children.

22

Mass Incarceration and Small Business

Bob Pelshaw

Bob Pelshaw is a formerly incarcerated author and entrepreneur. He is the founder of the National Campaign to Hire the Formerly Incarcerated and the author of Illegal to Legal: Business Success for the (Formerly) Incarcerated *and the forthcoming* Re-entry Success. *He was convicted of a felony related to the misuse of loan proceeds. He proposes to provide incarcerated individuals access to financial education, professional development, and mentorship tools to show them how to use their "street skills" to create legitimate sources of revenue to reduce the rates of recidivism.*

It is a tragedy that 89 percent of all recidivists don't have a job when they are re-arrested.[1] But we know employment lowers a person's chance of returning to prison. People returning from incarceration who also held stable employment for the first year had only a 16 percent chance of recidivism.[2]

Small business start-ups writ large have slowed over the last four decades.[3] The decline of small business startups reveals a tremendous opportunity to revive entrepreneurialism while reducing recidivism. Helping the formerly incarcerated start businesses could create a legal income stream and enterprises that could hire other people returning from incarceration—all while bolstering good ol' fashioned American entrepreneurialism.

Incarcerated people often talk about "the hustle," that is, whatever crime they did to make money outside, and even the things they do to improve their life inside prison. In conversations I had with various incarcerated and formerly incarcerated people, I learned that what separated the "hustler" and "entrepreneur" was rather small, the difference being only a matter of the right opportunities, guidance, and commitment.

Make "The Hustle" a Business

I know how to turn a hustle into a small business. I've owned several successful—and some not-so-successful—businesses over the years. I learned some of the best lessons in business inadvertently from my mom, who raised me and my six siblings by herself on welfare in a mixed-race household. She taught us all how to make something from nothing. Despite never earning more than $500 a month, she owned a comfortable home with air-conditioning, cable TV, and a freezer that was usually full of food—until she helped neighbors in need. From an early age I worked a paper route, raked leaves, and sometimes cleaned or painted houses for the little old ladies in our neighborhood. My "hustles" taught me a good work ethic and skills I used to launch other businesses.

Even though I was the youngest of seven, I was the first to receive a high school diploma, the first to go to college, and the first to become successfully self-employed. Over the years, I invested in, did site acquisition for, and consulted numerous businesses including laundromats, regional and national retail stores, office buildings, self-storage facilities, apartment complexes, hotels, hair salons, a car wash, and a restaurant. I was also the first in my family to make and lose a multi-million-dollar business empire and go to federal prison.

Yes, I know how to work my "hustle." My problem was that sometimes I hustled too hard. In my desire to get ahead, I occasionally pushed the envelope. I talked or negotiated my way out of problems, and things usually worked out. If you do that enough, you get used to functioning that way, especially when you reap the rewards. Unfortunately, I sometimes pushed the envelope in ways that didn't agree with my moral or ethical beliefs. In 2009, during the Great Recession, I went too far and broke the law by stupidly and temporarily misusing loan funds, causing me to receive a felony conviction and an all-expense stay at Leavenworth Federal Prison Camp. The hardest part about it was that I knew better. My actions cost me greatly.

Many of the men I met and served time with at Leavenworth dreamed of owning their own businesses, but drug dealing was the only model of self-employment most knew. If you can make money illegally as a profitable drug dealer, then you probably have the life skills to operate a legal business. You just need to be shown how to harness and channel the skills and dreams you already have.

I have a close relative who served time for distributing marijuana. After his release, I helped him start a laundry business that grew to three locations and included two commercial rental properties. "I used to think that the drug business was easy money," he told me. "It's faster to start, but harder to maintain or grow. But I now see that legal business is slower to start, but much easier in the long run than an illegal business."

During my incarceration, I learned it's easy to lose hope while in prison. It's even harder to maintain hope after prison, especially as society continues to punish convicts by not hiring us for jobs we are qualified for even after we've paid our debts. Without hope, it's impossible to have a vision for a different future. Without hope, there is no reason or desire to change. Even the Bible says, "Where there is no vision, the people perish."[4] Perhaps the lack of hope, precipitating a failure to change, is what could be driving our dismally high recidivism rate.

The last forty years of mass incarceration have proven that you can't necessarily legislate a person's desire to change. Getting older doesn't always help either. It has been said that age begets wisdom, but sometimes age arrives alone! Without hope or vision for something different, you return to what you know, even if it risks incarceration, or worse. It's hard to convince a person who was successful selling drugs to be excited to work at the seemingly low-paying jobs available to someone with a criminal history. Sadly, many go back to their old lives because they don't believe they can make a living legitimately, even knowing the risks returning to illegal activity carries.

Most of the guys I served time with dreamed of owning their own legal business, but they didn't have a vision of how to do it. They weren't looking to create the next Silicon Valley start-up. They simply wanted to be sole proprietors, like contractors, or have a lawn service or janitorial service—respectable businesses they could start on their own, either full-time or on the side as they temporarily worked a regular job. They dreamed of businesses they could start without a bank loan, which most couldn't get because of a lack of employment history, credit, or a clean background check. They wanted businesses they could start without an investor, because most didn't have the experience to gain investor confidence.

Out of everyone in prison, my hustle may have been the nerdiest of them all: I helped people write business plans and résumés. While I was incarcerated, I looked for resources to help someone start their own small business, but what I found was too complex or wasn't useful to the unique challenges facing returning citizens. I did find material about how to start a tech company, launch an IPO, or write a business plan—all written for a college-educated person and not relevant to the demographic of a typical prison.

Since being released, I have loved developing materials to help the incarcerated, formerly incarcerated, and those at risk of being incarcerated create income streams for themselves that don't involve returning to crime. It's not always about starting a small business either, as most people must work a job to fulfill terms of their probation or parole. I am passionate about helping people have better lives by creating and growing legitimate income streams, even if it's not something that would excite an investor or a banker.

Before I was incarcerated, I never hired anyone with a criminal past. After witnessing the talent I ignored firsthand, I set about trying to come up with material that would've convinced me to hire the right job applicant who just happened to have a criminal history. I started the National Campaign to Hire the Formerly Incarcerated to provide free resources for employers to help them hire citizens with a criminal history, as well as provide support for job applicants with criminal backgrounds.[5] I've spoken to returning citizens who said that they wouldn't consider working at a menial job, but I've convinced them to do so temporarily to gain a foundation to start their own business later. While I can't give people vision, I can try to give them hope, and hopefully I can show them a path they can take with their newfound hope. We need to open people's minds to possibilities that may help them envision a new future for themselves.

Real Change

I've been self-employed most of my life, to the point where now I would probably make a rotten employee. I think anyone who has been self-employed (legally or illegally) shares that same fate. I remember the line from John Milton's epic poem *Paradise Lost*, penned in the voice of Lucifer: "Better to reign in hell than serve in Heav'n."[6] Unfortunately, the streets and prison don't teach the social skills most employers require to advance in a career. However, the streets and prison do teach their denizens essential survival skills and can spark the hustle needed to launch and grow a business.

Starting a business isn't easy and isn't for everyone. I don't sugarcoat how difficult it is to successfully employ oneself as an entrepreneur. I feel like a broken record when I tell people that starting a business may be one of the hardest things they will ever do. However, I regularly visit prisons and jails and tell my incarcerated brothers and sisters that if they can survive prison, they can survive and do anything! That includes getting a job and starting a business.

Organizations like the Prison Entrepreneurship Program (PEP), RISE!, Determination Incorporated, 2nd Opportunity, LLC, and others have made great strides, but more needs to be done to train incarcerated citizens on how to use their life skills and passions to become entrepreneurs.[7]

If returning citizens are given the tools while incarcerated to become business owners, the economic potential they hold includes benefits well beyond the incarceration costs. Such an empowered person may finally be able to restart their child support payments, get off SNAP support, pay income taxes, and so on. Baylor University studied the PEP program and was able to show that a rehabilitated inmate, whether or not a business owner, brings a net return of $11,127 the first year after incarceration, and an ongoing savings of $10,042 per year or more thereafter.[8] Extrapolating these savings over a three-year period, a rehabilitated person contributes $28.50 to the economy daily for every day they spend outside prison. Tapping the potential of creating more entrepreneurs from formerly incarcerated citizens increases those returns exponentially, especially if the businesses created hire formerly incarcerated citizens.

People have nothing but time when they are inside. Once they hit the door, most can only afford to be concerned with survival. The best time to reach this group is while they are still incarcerated, or perhaps even before they enter prison. I believe simple steps are the most effective ones. Across the country, we can provide returning citizens the tools for a new future by doing the following:

1. *Offering practical small business training, along with employment and résumé-writing training, in prisons, jails, schools, and community groups.* As much as possible, these should be taught by formerly incarcerated people to create greater impact. Even if someone isn't going to start their own business, having this training could give them hope and a feeling of possibility. It might encourage some who might've ended up back on the streets to seek legal employment while they prepare to start a business.

2. *Being creative about new partnerships and new ways to work with existing financial support groups already teaching business and job skills.* A great example is the Georgetown Pivot Program, which is a fellowship for formerly incarcerated individuals that provides a one-year transition and reentry program with a non-credit-bearing certificate in business and entrepreneurship.[9] This collaborative program is a model partnership between local government and university entities that blends academic work and supported employment. Or the Homecoming Project in Alameda County, California, that matches returning citizens with homeowners who will rent to them, but they cover their rent for six months—kind of a charitable Airbnb model.[10]

3. *Recruiting mentors and support groups for returning citizens.* Returning citizens desperately need positive community involvement and support to succeed—we all know the importance of "networks." The very nature of LinkedIn is to connect people with similar interests and create economic opportunity. Unfortunately, most incarcerated people have networks that are not necessarily beneficial. By creating opportunities for people inside to be mentored by successful people on the outside, we can help them build a new network. Such support can lead to inroads for funding, business advice, and accountability that people who have never been to prison take for granted. Yet it could become the most important bridge between incarceration and productive citizenship.

4. *Helping the incarcerated, formerly incarcerated, and corrections staff find their strengths and talents.* Our justice system, and society at large, tends to focus on what is wrong with people who become and are justice-involved. Instead, we can give incarcerated and formerly incarcerated people the tools they need to know what's *right* with them. Include the CliftonStrengths and Builder Profile 10 assessments in the case files of every incarcerated citizen so they know their specific talents and assets. That alone could be revelatory for those who may have never heard anything positive about themselves in their lives. This will help people learn how to focus on positive outcomes. Self-knowledge of strengths and talents can help people succeed in employment and new businesses. It's no different than a corporation

using these tools to improve their employee's level of work. The more we prepare those inside prison with the same methods we use for those outside, the more we remove the barriers that keep them separate. Most incarcerated citizens eventually leave jail or prison, but the corrections staff are serving a life sentence—at least until they face job burnout and quit. It's no wonder that the corrections industry faces daunting recruitment and retention challenges, contributing to understaffing at many facilities. Insisting that the staff of every correctional facility engage in those same assessments could give the correctional system the tools it needs to help improve staffing and retention. If the staff were aware of the incarcerated residents' strengths and weaknesses, they could perhaps use that knowledge to help lead them in ways to reduce disciplinary and safety issues while building positive attributes in their populations that could better prepare them for successful reentry. If a person knows their strengths and weaknesses by the time they are released, that could maybe guide them into decisions that enhance their giftedness, instead of trap them in their weaknesses.

5. *Providing microloans and microgrants for well-prepared returning members who are looking to start sole proprietorships.* Funding groups that already provide training would be an excellent way to ensure returning citizens secure microloans and microgrants. Perhaps the Small Business Administration or banks could develop streamlined microloans that accommodate the lack of employment

caused by incarceration, along with accommodating for weaker credit, background checks, and so on.

6. *Encouraging employers to be more open about hiring the right candidate with a criminal history.* We urge the business owners and hiring managers we know to consider recruiting a qualified formerly incarcerated citizen. We can begin by demonstrating the benefit to their bottom line and the protections employers can receive by giving the right candidate a second chance.

These efforts would collectively expand what society believes is possible for the formerly incarcerated. With this perspective, we would then see in this population innovators, changemakers, and entrepreneurs who might apply what they have learned from their mistakes toward a positive, generative effort to change.

Wouldn't it be amazing if society's underdogs—formerly incarcerated and returning citizens—saved entrepreneurship in America by starting thousands of new businesses? What if the formerly incarcerated, and those at risk of being incarcerated—the very ones who are a fiscal drain on the system—became self-employed and hired workers that are denied by other companies? We could save more than money. We could save the innovation, independence, and work ethic that truly make America great, curtailing recidivism in the process.

23

A New North Star

DeAnna Hoskins

DeAnna Hoskins is president and CEO of JustLeadershipUSA. She is a formerly incarcerated person and a nationally recognized leader with experience as an advocate and policy expert at the local, state, and federal levels. Hoskins was formerly a senior policy advisor at the U.S. Department of Justice, and deputy director of the Federal Interagency Reentry Council. She calls for a renewed focus on human dignity in the justice reform movement.

What comes to mind when you think of trees, green lawns, and indoor plants? What setting would you assume contains a safe play area and an outdoor deck where people can connect with family and friends? A beautiful private home or community center, perhaps? Most people would associate these features with a place designed to help human beings live comfortably and thrive.

Would you believe that what I just described is what I saw when I visited prisons in Germany and Norway? In these countries, when children want to see their incarcerated parents, they are not forced to undergo body searches, metal detector tests, or harsh treatment (as if being the child of a person in prison is a crime). Children are brought in through discreet entrances that keep them from seeing the rest of the prison—as if they are just going to Dad's house. In stark contrast, families in the U.S. must endure stress and abuse to maintain contact with an incarcerated loved one—think long trips to faraway institutions where they are met with delays, invasive searches, and microaggressions, followed by a short visit under the watchful eye of an often hostile corrections officer.

A delegation of American criminal justice reform advocates and corrections professionals observed alternative approaches to confinement firsthand during an expedition sponsored by the Vera Institute for Justice.[1] I was part of a group of formerly incarcerated people who were invited to participate in a tour of four prisons in Europe. We witnessed a corrections model that is diametrically opposed to the U.S. criminal punishment system, prioritizing family reunification and other positive reinforcements that will help incarcerated people thrive once they are released. Men and women who commit crimes in Norway and Germany lose their physical liberty, but not their dignity. They live in clean and modern facilities where "normality" is the goal. They have access to quality medical care, educational and recreational opportunities, and private time with their families. Their human rights are strictly observed. The German corrections professionals we spoke to discussed their county's reckoning with the sins of the Holocaust and how their criminal justice approach today is part of a national process of collective healing, implemented to make sure that such a betrayal of human rights never happens again in Germany.

American prisons, on the other hand, are all about stripping people of their dignity. From the moment they begin to serve their disproportionately long sentences to the moment they leave with little more than the clothes on their back, people who go through the U.S. criminal punishment system are treated as if they are less than human. Some of the largest prisons in the U.S. are actually situated on former slave plantations.[2] These landmarks serve as painful reminders that, in the United States, we have not yet reckoned with our nation's original sins—Native American genocide and chattel slavery. From these atrocities, we can draw a straight line to our jails and prisons, filled with black and brown bodies—the remnants of a slave society. Fundamental change is not possible until our country confronts its past, goes through a process of truth and reconciliation, and repairs the harm.

Until the United States has systems for public safety that never require confinement, we must find humane alternatives to cages and brutality in our jails, detention centers, prisons, and all other secured facilities. I met a man in a Norwegian prison who said whenever he gets depressed he watches a documentary about U.S. prisons and thanks God he is in Norway.

As a formerly incarcerated woman and president of JustLeadershipUSA, an organization that centers the voices of those most harmed by criminal punishment and structural inequity, I have seen a new North Star from a distance. Generating a system that is truly grounded in justice requires that we treat all people with dignity and that we honor their human and constitutional rights. While some incremental remedies are needed to stop the bleeding, we must be careful to avoid getting trapped in the weeds of reform. We should offer education and direct services to the incarcerated and support them upon their release. We have a moral imperative to drastically improve conditions of confinement. However, we must also keep our eyes on the big prize—decarceration.

At JustLeadershipUSA we join others in the push toward decarceration by creating opportunities for self-actualization, self-advocacy, and civic engagement. Other organizations provide education and services both in prison and after release. These approaches are not in conflict with each other. They all support decarceration by lifting people up and helping them build communities, in the hopes that fewer of those people will get caught in a carceral cycle fueled by unjust policy and bad practice. These methods also reverse the harm done to individuals who have been entangled in systems that focus on punishment rather than reasonable measures of accountability. Accountability becomes possible when human dignity is centered in the process. Accountability opens the door to redemption, but that door swings both ways. The U.S. must also pursue its own redemption if we are to create a society of "liberty and justice for all."

There is an appetite for change in this country. One of the U.S. corrections officers who traveled with us to Germany and Norway, Commissioner Scott Semple from Connecticut, shared that Connecticut used to have a maximum-security prison—twenty-three-hour lockdown—in which violence was rampant among eighteen- to twenty-five-year-olds. Realizing that a dramatic shift in culture was essential, Commissioner Semple worked with Vera to create the TRUE* unit.[3] This unit replicates a model he learned during a previous trip to Germany. Inmates with life sentences, in the role of mentors, live in a housing unit with eighteen- to twenty-five-year-olds (emerging adults) where, instead of being locked down twenty-three hours a day, they are free sixteen hours a day. They have autonomy of movement within the unit and can choose from a variety of classes and programs to attend. A unit that traditionally held 300 people was repurposed to house 150 people including the mentors.[4] The other cells were converted into recreational space for reading, studying, meditation, and games. The TRUE unit has been operating for two years, and there has not yet been a single incidence of violence. Officials in South Carolina are preparing to replicate TRUE in one of its women's prisons.[5]

I remain hopeful that we will start making swift and bold progress throughout the U.S. I am compelled to hope. I am writing this essay while my son is unjustly caught up in a system because he faces unreasonable parole conditions and a judge who believes harsh punishment is the only remedy for a parole violation. My son is caged in a state replete with overt, systemic racism. I cannot stop now. Every young man who is incarcerated reminds me of my son, my cousins, my uncle. The thread of incarceration is woven through the fabric of

---

* TRUE stands for Truthfulness, Respectfulness, Understanding, and Elevating.

my family. Even my mother's brother was killed in a Macon, Georgia, prison by guards in the '60s.

I don't have any wonky policy solutions. I have only an urgent plea for human dignity to become the foundation upon which we build a society that believes in its own need for redemption, is willing to be held accountable for the harm it has caused, and extends that same opportunity to two million incarcerated people, forty-one million people under probation and parole, and seventy million people with criminal record histories who currently reside in the "land of free and the home of the brave."[6] Human dignity, national accountability—that is our North Star. The movement, led by those who have been doused in the undammed river of systemic oppression flowing from Native American genocide through slavery and Reconstruction, through Jim Crow, ghettoization, and mass criminalization, will be our guide as we reach for that star.

Acknowledgments

Many people came together to make this project a reality. First and foremost, thank you to the hundreds of authors who shared their personal stories and insightful reform ideas with us. The essays contained in this book represent only a sliver of those that were sent to us. We received an incredibly diverse array of submissions from people across the country—many of whom are currently incarcerated. We were overwhelmed by the responses we received and astounded by the strength and power of your contributions. We believe you are the leaders who will make all the difference in the fight for a more fair, just, and equitable criminal justice system.

This book would not be possible were it not for the support of the team at the Center for American Progress (CAP). Thank you to Lea Hunter, who spent countless hours reading and rereading hundreds of submissions and bringing this book to life. Our sincere thanks to Ed Chung, whose leadership was integral to taking this project from just an idea to the book that you hold today. We'd like to express our sincere gratitude to the rest of the CAP team: Betsy Pearl, Maritza Perez, Allison Young, Azza Altiraifi, Olugbenga Ajilore, David Ballard, Rukmani Bhatia, Kyle Epstein, Bayliss Fiddiman, Anthony

Hanna, Laura Jimenez, Shabab Mirza, Caitlin Rooney, and Jessica Yin.

Finally, thank you to Diane Wachtell, our editor and publisher, who first conceived of a book of reform ideas from justice-involved individuals. Along with Kameel Mir and the rest of her team at The New Press, Diane supported this book before we even understood what it would become. Thank you for your patience and careful attention to detail. This was a learning process for us, and you were an invaluable thought partner in helping us reach the finish line.

Notes

Introduction

1. Wendy Sawyer and Peter Wagner, "Mass Incarceration: The Whole Pie 2019," Prison Policy Initiative, March 19, 2019, www.prisonpolicy.org/reports/pie2019.html; The Sentencing Project, "Criminal Justice Facts," www.sentencingproject.org/criminal-justice-facts; The Sentencing Project, "Incarcerated Women and Girls," June 6, 2019, www.sentencingproject.org/publications/incarcerated-women-and-girls; Anastasia Christman and Michelle Natividad Rodriguez, "Research Supports Fair Chance Policies," National Employment Law Project, August 1, 2016, www.nelp.org/publication/research-supports-fair-chance-policies.

2. All of Us or None of Us, "Ban the Box Timeline," www.prisonerswithchildren.org/wp-content/uploads/2015/08/BTB-timeline-final.pdf; Beth Avery, "Ban the Box: U.S. Cities, Counties, and States Adopt Fair Hiring Policies," National Employment Law Project, July 1, 2019, www.nelp.org/publication/ban-the-box-fair-chance-hiring-state-and-local-guide.

3. Florida Rights Restoration Coalition, "About Desmond Meade," https://floridarrc.com/desmond-meade.

4. Bryan Stevenson, *Just Mercy* (New York: Random House, 2014), 17–18.

1. Earmark Jobs to Reduce Recidivism

1. Lucious Couloute and Daniel Kopf, "Out of Prison & Out of Work: Unemployment Among Formerly Incarcerated People," Prison Policy Initiative, July 2018, www.prisonpolicy.org/reports/outofwork.html.

2. A Tiny Ray of Light: On the Need for an Authentic Oversight Regime Within the Texas Department of Criminal Justice

1. Sontag, Susan, *Regarding the Pain of Others* (London: Penguin Books, 2005), 100.

2. See Texas Department of Criminal Justice, "Administrative Review & Management Division," www.tdcj.texas.gov/divisions/arrm /res_grievance.html.

3. Prison Litigation Reform Act of 1995, Public Law 104-134, *U.S. Statutes at Large* 110 (1996). See also ACLU, "Know Your Rights: The Prison Litigation Reform Act (PLRA)," www.aclu.org/sites/default/files /images/asset_upload_file79_25805.pdf.

4. Matt Clarke, "State Auditor: Texas Prisoners Face Retaliation for Airing Grievances," *Prison Legal News*, May 15, 2009, www .prisonlegalnews.org/news/2009/may/15/state-auditor-texas-prisoners -face-8232retaliation-for-airing-grievances.

5. Office of the State Auditor, Texas, *An Audit Report on the Department of Criminal Justice's Complaint Resolution and Investigation Functions*, September 2008, 2.

6. Office of the State Auditor, 2.

7. Office of the State Auditor, 9.

8. Office of the State Auditor, 16.

9. Office of the State Auditor, Texas, "Summary of Report 009-004," September 2008, www.sao.texas.gov/SAOReports/Report Number?id=09-004.

10. Texas Department of Criminal Justice, ARRM Division, *Ombudsman Resolution Report Fiscal Year 2017*, www.tdcj.texas.gov/documents /Ombudsman_Report_FY2017.pdf.

11. Texas Department of Criminal Justice, ARRM Division, 2–24.

12. Keri Blakinger, "4 Texas Prison Officials Indicted after Alleged Screwdriver-Planting Incident at Brazoria Lockup," *Houston Chronicle*, July 11, 2018, www.chron.com/news/houston-texas/article/4-Texas -prison-officials-indicted-after-alleged-13064474.php.

13. "Texas Prison Officials Demoted, Fired after Disciplinary Quota System and Planted Contraband Exposed," *Prison Legal News*, November 6, 2018, www.prisonlegalnews.org/news/2018/nov/6/texas-prison -officials-demoted-fired-after-disciplinary-quota-system-and-planted -contraband-exposed.

14. See Human Rights Watch, "United States Ratification of International Human Rights Treaties," July 24, 2009, www.hrw.org/news/2009

/07/24/united-states-ratification-international-human-rights-treaties.

15. Wade Godwyn, "Texas Governor Deploys State Guard to Stave Off Obama Takeover," NPR, May 2, 2015, www.npr.org/sections /itsallpolitics/2015/05/02/403865824/texas-governor-deploys-state -guard-to-stave-off-obama-takeover.

16. Hannah Wiley, "Advocates Say the Timing Is Right for Independent Oversight of Texas Prisons," *Texas Tribune*, November 26, 2018, www.texastribune.org/2018/11/26/advocates-say-time -right-independent-oversight-texas-prisons/.

17. Texas Department of Criminal Justice, "Fiscal Year 2019 Operating Budget, Fiscal Years 2020–2021 Legislative Appropriations Request," Texas Department of Criminal Justice, August 24, 2018, www.tdcj.texas.gov /documents/bfd/Operating_Budget_FY2019_LAR_Summary_FY2020 -21.pdf; see Juleyka Lantigua-Williams, "7,000 Deaths in Custody," *The Atlantic*, July 28, 2018, www.theatlantic.com/politics/archive/2016/07 /7000-deaths-in-custody-texas/493325/.

18. See Independent Monitoring Boards, "About Us," www.imb.org .uk/about-us/.

3. Unlock Digital Inclusion

1. Rich McCormick, "Watch Steve Jobs Introduce the iPhone 10 Years Ago," January 9, 2017, www.theverge.com/2017/1/9/14208974/iphone -announcement-10-year-anniversary-steve-jobs.

2. "Barriers to Work: People with Criminal Records," National Conference of State Legislatures, July 17, 2018, www.ncsl.org/research /labor-and-employment/barriers-to-work-individuals-with-criminal -records.aspx.

3. The National Inventory of Collateral Consequences of Conviction (NICCC) catalogues the legal and regulatory restrictions that are imposed on individuals convicted of crimes across state and federal statutory and regulatory codes. At this writing, the NICCC included over forty-four thousand consequences. See Council of State Governments Justice Center, "National Inventory of Collateral Consequences of Conviction," https://niccc.csgjusticecenter.org/.

4. For an in-depth overview of the impact of collateral consequences, see U.S. Commission on Civil Rights, "Collateral Consequences: the Crossroads of Punishment, Redemption, and the Effects on Communities," June 2019, www.usccr.gov/pubs/2019/06-13-Collateral -Consequences.pdf.

5. Nikita Singareddy, "Former Prisoners Rethink Criminal Justice Through Entrepreneurship and Civic Technology," *TechCrunch*, September 4, 2015, https://techcrunch.com/2015/09/04/former-prisoners-rethink-criminal-justice-through-entrepreneurship-and-civic-technology/.

6. "Let's Talk About Digital Inclusion," Orange, www.orange.com/en/Human-Inside/Mag/Let-s-talk-about-digital-inclusion.

7. Meagan Wilson, Rayane Alamuddin, and Danielle Cooper, *Unbarring Access: A Landscape Review of Postsecondary Education in Prison and Its Pedagogical Supports*, Ithaka S+R, May 30, 2019, https://sr.ithaka.org/publications/landscape-review-postsecondary-education-in-prison/.

8. "NRRC Facts and Trends," The National Reentry Resource Center, https://csgjusticecenter.org/nrrc/facts-and-trends/.

9. Philip Bulman, "Using Technology to Make Prisons and Jails Safer," National Institute of Justice, www.nij.gov/journals/262/pages/corrections-technology.aspx.

10. Araba Sey, Chris Coward, François Bar, George Skiadas, Chris Rothschild, and Lucas Koepke, *Connecting People for Development: Why Public Access ICTs Matter*, University of Washington Information School, 2013; Harvard Health Letter, "5 Ways the Internet Can Help You Boost Your Health," June 2016, www.health.harvard.edu/staying-healthy/5-ways-the-internet-can-help-you-boost-your-health.

11. Kristina Ericksen, "5 IT Certifications That Will Help Launch Your Tech Career," *Technology Blog*, Rasmussen College, March 19, 2018, www.rasmussen.edu/degrees/technology/blog/5-it-certifications-to-get-your-foot-in-the-door.

12. Society for Human Resource Management, "Background Checking—The Use of Criminal Background Checks in Hiring Decisions" (2012), p. 2, www.shrm.org/research/surveyfindings/articles/pages/criminalbackgroundcheck.aspx.

13. Criminal justice reformer Eddie Ellis highlighted the significance of person-first terminology in his now well-known "language letter." See Eddie Ellis, "An Open Letter to Our Friends on the Question of Language," Center for NuLeadership on Urban Solutions, 2007, https://static1.squarespace.com/static/58eb0522e6f2e1dfce591dee/t/596e13f48419c2e5a0e95d30/1500386295291/CNUS-language-letter-2016.pdf.

14. In 2018, a national strike attempted to call attention to these conditions. See Molly Olmstead, "Prisoners Launch National 19-Day Strike to Protest Unpaid Labor and Poor Prison Conditions," *Slate*, August 21, 2018.

4. On Prison Labor

1. U.S. Constitution, amend. 13, sec. 1.

2. Michael J. Sandel, *Justice: What's the Right Thing to Do?* (New York: Farrar, Straus, and Giroux, 2009), 201–2.

3. Sandel, *Justice*, 124.

4. Sandel, 121–23.

5. Sandel, 121–23.

6. *Vanskike v. Peters*, 974 F.2d 806, 809 (7th Cir., 1992); see Fair Labor Standards Act, U.S. Code 29 (2019), Section 201 and what follows.

7. *Vanskike v. Peters.*

8. Shane Bauer, *American Prison: A Reporter's Undercover Journey into the Business of Punishment* (New York: Penguin Books, 2018), 19–22.

9. Bauer, *American Prison*, 196, 246.

10. *Hammond v. Collier*, Civil Action No. H-16-3603 (S.D. Tex., Mar. 31, 2017).

11. *Hammond v. Collier*. See *Ali v. Johnson*, 259 F.3d 317, 318 (5th Cir., 2001): *Murray v. Miss. Dep't of Corr.*, 911 F.2d 1167 (5th Cir., 1990).

12. *Loving v. Johnson*, 455 F.3d 562, 563 (5th Cir., 2006).

13. *Mikeska v. Collins*, 900 F.2d 833, 837 (5th Cir., 1990), modified, 928 F.2d 126 (5th Cir. 1991).

14. Wendy Sawyer, "How Much Do Incarcerated People Earn in Each State?," Prison Policy Initiative, April 10, 2017, www.prisonpolicy.org /blog/2017/04/10/wages.

15. See Florida Statute XLVII (2019), 944.275.

16. See Ashurst-Sumners Act of 1935, U.S. Code 18 (2019), Sections 1761–62.

17. U.S. Code 18 (2019), Section 4124.

18. See also Nathan James, "Federal Prison Industries: Overview and Legislative History" Congressional Research Service, www.hsdl.org /?abstract&did=731931.

19. David Reutter, "Prisoner Labor Focus of Controversy in Texas, Alabama," *Prison Legal News*, October 10, 2017, www.prisonlegalnews.org /news/2017/oct/10/prisoner-labor-focus-controversy-texas-alabama.

20. Tara Herivel and Paul Wright, eds., *Prison Profiteers: Who Makes Money from Mass Incarceration* (New York: The New Press, 2007).

21. Anne Applebaum, *Gulag* (New York: Doubleday, 2003).

5. Correcting Excessive Sentences of Youthful Offenders

1. See Government Code 508.001, in *Vernon's Annotated Code of Criminal Procedure of the State of Texas* (Kansas City, MO: Vernon Law Book Co., 1989).

2. American Civil Liberties Union of Texas and Texas Civil Rights Project-Houston, "A Solitary Failure: The Waste, Cost and Harm of Solitary Confinement in Texas," 36, www.prisonlegalnews.org /media/publications/A%20Solitary%20Failure%20TX%20Solitary%20 Report%20ACLU%202015.pdf.

3. See Chai Woodham, "Eastern State Penitentiary: A Prison with a Past," *Smithsonian*, September 30, 2008, www.smithsonianmag.com /history/eastern-state-penitentiary-a-prison-with-a-past-14274660/.

4. The issues described here are exemplified by the passage and legacy of the Violent Crime Control Act and Law Enforcement Act of 1994, better known as "the 1994 crime bill." See Carrie Johnson, "20 Years Later, Parts of Major Crime Bill Viewed as Terrible Mistake," *NPR Morning Edition*, September 12, 2014.

5. House Research Organization, "Mandatory Supervision Release: Safety, Cost and Legal Issues," *Session Focus*, Texas State House of Representatives, February 17, 1997, hro.house.texas.gov/pdf/focus/mandsu.pdf.

6. See National Research Council, The Growth of Incarceration in the United States: Exploring Causes and Consequences (Washington, DC: National Academies Press, 2014).

7. "Criminal Justice Facts," The Sentencing Project, www .sentencingproject.org/criminal-justice-facts/.

8. See Texas Department of Criminal Justice "Parole Division," www.tdcj.texas.gov/divisions/pd/specialized_programs.html.

6. An Act to Increase Voter Registration and Participation

1. People incarcerated in prison as pretrial detainees or for civil commitments are allowed to vote by absentee ballot in Massachusetts. Maine and Vermont are the only U.S. states that allow all incarcerated citizens to vote. See Emancipation Initiative, "Timeline of Massachusetts Incarcerated Voting Rights," http://emancipationinitiative.org /ballots-over-bars/returning-the-right-to-vote.

2. The African American Coalition Committee began as the Black Rights Committee, which was founded here in MCI-Norfolk in September of 1972. The author is currently the vice-chairman of the AACC.

3. There are only fourteen states, one of which is Massachusetts,

that return the right to vote immediately upon release. If this measure were adopted elsewhere, in some states (e.g., Alaska, Arkansas, Georgia) ex-offenders would have to wait through the duration of their sentence, including probation or parole, before they could be registered. In other states (e.g., California, Colorado, Connecticut), only parole must be completed before they are registered. Those who live in states with permanent disenfranchisement (Kentucky) or that permanently disenfranchise offenders for specific crimes (e.g., Alabama, Arizona, Delaware) will of course not be allowed to register.

4. Just in the state of Massachusetts alone, most of the approximately 9,800 people incarcerated in county jails and houses of correction can vote by absentee ballot—as long as they are at least eighteen years old, are U.S. citizens, and are not incarcerated for felony convictions or voter fraud. However, the implementation of new policy is necessary because many jails and houses of correction across the state do not help incarcerated people obtain absentee ballots, and in fact some give false information on people's eligibility to vote. Even when incarcerated people have the funds and knowledge to request an absentee ballot, some town clerks illegally reject these ballots, leaving incarcerated people with little recourse. Emancipation Initiative, "Timeline."

5. Christopher Uggen and Jeff Manda, "Voting and Subsequent Crime and Arrest: Evidence from a Community Sample," *Columbia Human Rights Law Review* 36 (2004): 193–215, https://pdfs.semanticscholar.org/3887/bffdb10e5006e2f902fcf2a46abaa9efdf46.pdf.

6. Bill HB 669, "Increasing Voter Registration and Participation to Help Prevent Recidivism," The 191st General Court of the Commonwealth of Massachusetts, malegislature.gov/Bills/191/H669.

7. Emancipation Initiative, "Timeline."

8. Massachusetts Department of Correction, "Prison Population Trends 2017," March 2018, www.mass.gov/files/documents/2018/09/28/PrisonPopTrends_2017_Final.pdf.

9. Boston Bar Association, "Unlock Democracy—Restoring Voting Rights to Incarcerated People," October 28, 2019, www.bostonbar.org/membership/events/event-details?ID=32941.

10. Nicole Lewis, "In Just Two States, All Prisoners Can Vote. Here's Why Few Do," The Marshall Project, June 11, 2019, www.themarshallproject.org/2019/06/11/in-just-two-states-all-prisoners-can-vote-here-s-why-few-do.

11. Massachusetts Department of Correction, "Quarterly Report on the Status of Prison Capacity, First Quarter 2017," April 2017, www.mass.gov/files/documents/2017/05/zm/2017-1stQtr-PrisonCapacity-Report.pdf.

12. National Conference of State Legislatures, "Felon Voting Rights," December 21, 2018, www.ncsl.org/research/elections-and-campaigns/felon-voting-rights.aspx.

7. On Honor Yards

1. Kenneth E. Hartman, *Mother California: A Story of Redemption Behind Bars* (New York: Atlas & Co., 2009).

2. Hartman, 171.

3. See Lynn Novick, *College Behind Bars* (film), https://www.pbs.org/kenburns/college-behind-bars, and also the Bard Prison Initiative website at https://bpi.bard.edu/our-work/the-college.

8. Undebatable

1. White House Council of Economic Advisors, *Economic Perspectives on Incarceration and the Criminal Justice System,* April 2016, www.obamawhitehouse.archives.gov/sites/default/files/page/files/20160423_cea_incarceration_criminal_justice.pdf, 24–27.

2. Lois M. Davis et al., *How Effective Is Correctional Education, and Where Do We Go from Here? The Results of a Comprehensive Evaluation* (Santa Monica, CA: RAND Corporation, 2014), www.rand.org/pubs/research_reports/RR564.html.

3. Ruth Delaney, Ram Subramanian, and Fred Patrick, "Making the Grade: Developing Quality Postsecondary Education Programs in Prison," Vera Institute of Justice, July 2016, www.vera.org/publications/making-the-grade-postsecondary-education-programs-in-prison.

4. See Daniel S. Throop, "The Inside Story of a Legendary Prison Debate Team," The Marshall Project, June 6, 2018.

5. "About the Prison Education Program," Boston University, http://sites.bu.edu/pep/about.

6. Charmaine Mercer, "Federal Pell Grants for Prisoners," Congressional Research Service, December 14, 2004.

7. As reported by the author. Similar programs of college programming in prisons report significantly lower recidivism rates. For example, New York Department of Correction Research Unit found a significant difference between program participants (7 percent) compared with non-participants (29 percent). See Jillian Baranger et al., "Doing Time Wisely: The Social and Personal Benefits of Higher Education in Prison," *The Prison Journal* 98, no. 4 (2018): 495.

8. White House Council of Economic Advisors, *Economic Perspectives,* 5.

9. "Who We Serve," Massachusetts Department of Corrections,

www.mass.gov/orgs/massachusetts-department-of-correction.

10. Gordon Haas, "Massachusetts Department of Correction," Norfolk Lifers Group, 2014, www.realcostofprisons.org/writing/haas-ma -doc-2014--july-2016.pdf.

11. Gordon Haas, "A Report on the DOC Expenditures and Staffing Levels for Fiscal Year 2015," Norfolk Lifers Group, November 2016, www.realcostofprisons.org/writing/haas-doc-spending-for-2015.pdf.

12. Haas, "A Report on the DOC Expenditures."

13. Mary Ellen Mastrorilli, Danielle Rousseau, and James Matesanz, "Higher Degrees: Liberal Arts Education Brings New Thinking," *Corrections Today*, July–August 2016.

14. James Matesanz, in letter to the author, January 30, 2017.

15. James Keown and Daniel Throop, *Corrective Lenses: A Rethinking of American Punishment Systems* (Holts Summit, MO: Quail Valley Publishing, 2014).

16. Natasha Haverty, "After Half a Century, Inmates Resurrect the Norfolk Prison Debating Society," *NPR Morning Edition*, December 27, 2016.

17. Haverty, "After Half a Century, Inmates Resurrect"; also Daniel S. Throop, "The Inside Story of a Legendary Prison Debate Team," The Marshall Project, June 7, 2019, www.themarshallproject.org/2018/06/07 /the-inside-story-of-a-legendary-prison-debate-team; and Jill Lepore, "Malcom X's Prison Debate Team Takes On Harvard," *New Yorker*, April 9, 2019.

9. A Call for Pardons

1. This practice continues. See https://www.hrw.org/news/2018/02/28/ us-freezing-cells-detained-migrants.

2. See "Governor Cuomo Grants Pardons," December 31, 2014, https://www.governor.ny.gov/news/governor-cuomo-grants-pardons.

3. See U.S. Immigration and Customs Enforcement, https://www.ice .gov/statistics.

4. Alex Nowrasteh, "Deportation Rates in Historical Perspective," Cato Institute, September 16, 2019, https://www.cato.org/blog /deportation-rates-historical-perspective; U.S. Department of Homeland Security, "Table 39. Aliens Removed or Returned: Fiscal Years 1892 to 2017," https://www.dhs.gov/immigration-statistics/yearbook /2017/table39.

5. American Immigration Council, "Fact Sheet: The Cost of Immigration Enforcement and Border Security," October 14, 2019, https://www.americanimmigrationcouncil.org/research/the-cost-of-immigration-enforcement-and-border-security.

6. "Illegal Immigration Reform and Immigrant Responsibility Act of 1996: Conference Report," https://www.congress.gov/104/crpt/hrpt828/CRPT-104hrpt828.pdf.

7. See Pamela Constable, "For Non-U.S. Citizens, Early Release from Prison Means Swift Deportation," *Washington Post*, November 5, 2015.

8. Elizabeth Rapaport, "The Georgia Immigration Pardons: A Case Study in Mass Clemency," *Federal Sentencing Reporter* 13, nos. 3–4 (2000): 184–87; Kirk Semple, "Panel Is Facing Deadline on Immigrants' Pardons," *New York Times*, October 21, 2010.

9. Kirk Semple, "Governor Pardons Six Immigrants Facing Deportation Over Old Crimes," *New York Times*, December 6, 2010.

10. Over-Incarceration and Gain Time: What's Wrong and How to Fix It

1. See National Research Council, *The Growth of Incarceration in the United States: Exploring Causes and Consequences* (Washington, DC: National Academies Press, 2014).

2. Pew Charitable Trusts, *Collateral Costs: Incarcerations Effect on Economic Mobility* (Washington, DC: Pew Charitable Trusts, 2010).

3. Florida Department of Corrections, *2017–18 Annual Report*, www.dc.state.fl.us/pub/annual/1718/FDC_AR2017-18.pdf.

4. Drew Wilson, "More Gain Time Could Cut Florida Prison Population," *Florida Politics*, March 28, 2019, https://floridapolitics.com/archives/292117-more-gain-time-could-cut-florida-prison-population.

11. From Coming Home to Running the Homecoming Project

1. See Homecoming Project at impactjustice.org/impact/homecoming-project.

2. Susan Turner et al., "Development of the Static Risk Assessment (CSRA): Recidivism Risk Prediction in the California Department of Corrections and Rehabilitation," Center for Evidence Based Corrections, September 2013, ucicorrections.seweb.uci.edu/files/2013/12/Development-of-the-CSRA-Recidivism-Risk-Prediction-in-the-CDCR.pdf.

3. Lucius Couloute, "Nowhere to Go: Homelessness Among Formerly Incarcerated People," Prison Policy Initiative, August 2018, www .prisonpolicy.org/reports/housing.html.

4. See Sharon Chin, "Program Connects Released Prison Inmates with Welcoming Homes in East Bay," *CBS SF BayArea*, February 2019, sanfrancisco.cbslocal.com/2019/02/28/program-connects-released -prison-inmates-with-welcoming-homes-in-east-bay.

12. "Life" Means Death

1. Charles Babington, "Glendening to Reject Parole in Life Sentences," *Washington Post*, September 22, 1995.

2. Frank Woolever, *Gandhi's List of Social Sins: Lessons in Truth* (Pittsburgh, PA: Dorrance Publishing, 2011).

3. ACLU, "False Hope: How Parole Systems Fail Youth Serving Extreme Sentences," November 2016, www.aclu.org/sites/default/files /field_document/121416-aclu-parolereportonlinesingle.pdf.

4. Walter Lomax and Sonia Kumar, *Still Blocking the Exit*, Maryland Restorative Justice Initiative and the American Civil Liberties Union of Maryland, January 2015, www.aclu-md.org/en/publications/still -blocking-exit; Angela Jacob and Associated Press, "Governor Should be Removed from Parole Process, Former Md. Gov. Says," NBC Washington, March 8, 2019, www.nbcwashington.com/news/local/Former-MD -Gov-Says--Should-be-Removed-from-Parole-Process-476271173.html.

13. The 13th and the Problem of the Color Line

1. William M. Carter Jr., "Thirteenth Amendment and Constitutional Change," *NYU Review of Law and Social Change* 38 (2014): 583, 587.

2. Frederick Douglass, "The Need For Continuing Anti-Slavery Work, speech at Thirty-Second Annual Meeting of the American Anti-Slavery Society," in *Frederick Douglass: Selected Speeches and Writings*, ed. Philip S. Foner, abridged and adapted by Yuval Taylor (Chicago, IL: 1999), 579.

3. Michael Hallett. "Commerce with Criminals: The New Colonialism in Criminal Justice," *Review of Policy Research* 21, no. 1 (2004): 53.

4. U.S. Congress, House, *An Act to Protect All Persons in the United States in their Civil Rights, and Furnish the Means of their Vindication*, 38th Cong., 1st sess., www.loc.gov/law/help/statutes-at-large/39th-congress /session-1/c39s1ch31.pdf.

5. Brett E. Garland, Cassia Spohn, and Eric J. Wodahl, "Racial Disproportionality in the American Prison Population: Using the Blumstein Method to Address the Critical Race and Justice Issue of the 21st Century," *Justice Policy Journal* 5, no. 2 (2008): 13–14.

6. See Jennifer, E. Bronson, Ann Carson, Bureau of Justice Statistics (BJS), U.S. Dept. of Justice, Office of Justice Programs, and United States of America, "Prisoners in 2017," *Age* 500 (2019): 400. Calculation includes number of sentenced federal prisoners and defines people of color as black, Hispanic, Asian, Native Hawaiian, Pacific Islander, American Indian, Alaska Native, and persons of two or more races.

7. See Marx Maxey, "Corporations and Governments Collude in Prison Slavery Racket," *People's World*, February 7, 2018, www .peoplesworld.org/article/corporations-and-governments-collude-in -prison-slavery-racket.

14. From the Ground Up: Tapping the Strengths of Incarcerated People

1. See U.S. Department of Education, "12,000 Incarcerated Students to Enroll in Postsecondary Educational and Training Programs Through Education Department's New Second Chance Pell Pilot Program," press release, June 24, 2016, www.ed.gov/news/press-releases /12000-incarcerated-students-enroll-postsecondary-educational-and -training-programs-through-education-departments-new-second -chance-pell-pilot-program.

2. Wendy Sawyer and Peter Wagner, "Mass Incarceration: The Whole Pie 2019," Prison Policy Initiative, March 19, 2019, www.prisonpolicy .org/reports/pie2019.html.

3. *Encyclopaedia Britannica Online*, s.v. "Mike Tyson, American Boxer," www.britannica.com/biography/Mike-Tyson.

4. Abigail Hess, "California Is Paying Inmates $1 an Hour to Fight Wildfires," *CNBC Make It*, November 12, 2018, www.cnbc.com/2018/08 /14/california-is-paying-inmates-1-an-hour-to-fight-wildfires.html.

15. A Bridge to Employment

1. Daniel Mkude, Lisbeth Levey and Brian Cooksey, *Higher Education in Tanzania: A Case Study* (Oxford/Dar es Salaam: Partnership for

Higher Education in Africa, 2003), 106–107; Chidinma Irene Nwoye, "African Countries Are Seeing a "Brain Gain" as Young Elite Graduates Give Up on the West," *Quartz Africa*, November 24, 2017, https://qz.com/africa/1128778/africa-brain-drain-to-brain-gain-african-elite-graduates-head-home-as-brexit-trump-eu-close-doors.

2. The choice to use "criminal legal system" versus "criminal justice system" is an acknowledgement that a system that hyper-targets black and brown people for arrest, conviction, incarceration, and indebtedness is not just, and "justice" has historically been absent, hindered, or deferred. The choice to replace it with "legal" acknowledges the law as the primary tool of the system.

3. Lumina Foundation, "Lumina State Policy Agenda 2017–2020," https://www.luminafoundation.org/files/resources/lumina-state-policy-agenda-2017-20-final.pdf.

16. Closing the Literacy Gap

1. CSG Justice Center, "Three Core Elements of Programs That Reduce Recidivism: Who, What, and How Well," July 7, 2015, csgjusticecenter.org/jr/posts/three-core-elements-of-programs-that-reduce-recidivism-who-what-and-how-well.

2. National Center for Education Statistics, "Literacy Domain," nces.ed.gov/surveys/piaac/literacy.asp.

3. Wendy Sawyer and Pete Wagner, "Mass Incarceration: The Whole Pie 2019," Prison Policy Initiative, March 19, 2019, www.prisonpolicy.org/reports/pie2019.html.

4. ExcelinEd, "Does K-3 Reading Matter? Ask the 70% of Inmates Who Can't Read," March 28, 2016, www.excelined.org/edfly-blog/does-k-3-reading-matter-ask-the-70-of-inmates-who-cant-read.

5. James Sterngold, "Illiteracy Reinforces Prisoners' Captivity," *San Francisco Chronicle*, December 27, 2006, www.sfgate.com/education/article/illiteracy-reinforces-prisoners-captivity-2464866.php.

6. Andrew Sum et al., *The Consequences of Dropping Out of High School: Joblessness and Jailing for High School Dropouts and the High Cost for Taxpayers*, Prison Policy Initiative, October 2009, www.prisonpolicy.org/scans/The_Consequences_of_Dropping_Out_of_High_School.pdf.

7. U.S. Department of Justice, Federal Bureau of Prisons, "Program Statement," December 1, 2003, www.bop.gov/policy/progstat/5350_028.pdf.

8. "Prison Designation," Prisonology, https://prisonologyx.com/preparation/prsion-designation/custody-level.

9. Adult Education Solutions, "TABE Test of Adult Basic Education," tabetest.com/PDFs/TABE_Overview_Brochure.pdf.

10. Bobby D. Rampey et al., "Highlights from the U.S. PIAAC Survey of Incarcerated Adults: Their Skills, Work Experience, Education, and Training: 2014," November 2016, https://nces.ed.gov/pubs2016/2016040.pdf.

11. First Step Act of 2018, Public Law 115-391, *U.S. Statutes at Large*, vol. 132 (Washington, DC: U.S. Government Publishing Office, 2018): 5193. See also "The First Step Act of 2018: An Overview," Congressional Research Service, fas.org/sgp/crs/misc/R45558.pdf.

12. "Data Collection: National Prisoner Statistics Program," Office of Justice Programs, Bureau of Justice Statistics, www.bjs.gov/index.cfm?ty=dcdetail&iid=269.

17. The Age of Inequality: Ending the Mass Incarceration of Our Youth

1. James Swift, "The Dreary State of Juvenile Mental Health Care, Inside and Outside the Justice System," Juvenile Justice Information Exchange, August 5, 2013, jjie.org/2013/08/05/the-dreary-state-of-juvenile-mental-health-care-inside-and-outside-the-justice-system.

2. Paul Elam and Francisco A. Villarruel, "A 17-year-old Is Not an Adult, and Shouldn't Be Treated as Such. Even Felons," Justice Policy Institute, May 19, 2017, www.justicepolicy.org/news/11430.

3. See Krista Larson and Hernan Carvente, "Juvenile Justice Systems Still Grappling with Legacy of the 'Superpredator' Myth," Vera Institute of Justice, January 24, 2017, www.vera.org/blog/juvenile-justice-systems-still-grappling-with-legacy-of-the-superpredator-myth.

4. Josh Rovner, "How Tough on Crime Became Tough on Kids: Prosecuting Teenage Drug Charges in Adult Courts," The Sentencing Project, December 7, 2016, www.sentencingproject.org/publications/tough-crime-became-tough-kids-prosecuting-teenage-drug-charges-adult-courts.

5. Jessica Lahey, "The Steep Costs of Keeping Juveniles in Adult Prisons," *The Atlantic*, January 8, 2016.

6. Heidi Washington, *2017 Statistical Report*, Michigan Department of Corrections, January 23, 2019, www.michigan.gov/documents

/corrections/MDOC_2017_Statistical_Report_644556_7.pdf, p. C-11.

7. Caitlin Curley, "Juveniles Tried as Adults: What Happens When Children Go to Prison," GenFKD, November 11, 2016, www.genfkd.org /juveniles-tried-adults-happens-children-go-prison.

8. Ted Roelofs, "Is Michigan's Criminal Justice System, One That Prosecutes Teens as Adults, Wasting 20,000 Lives and at What Expense?" *Bridge Magazine*, June 10, 2014, www.mlive.com/politics/2014 /06/is_michigan_wasting_20000_teen.html.

9. Wendy Sawyer, "Youth Confinement: The Whole Pie," Prison Policy Initiative, February 27, 2018, www.prisonpolicy.org/reports /youth2018.html.

10. Roelofs, "Michigan's Criminal Justice System."

11. Justice Policy Institute, *The Costs of Confinement: Why Good Juvenile Justice Policies Make Good Fiscal Sense*, May 2009, www.justicepolicy.org /images/upload/09_05_rep_costsofconfinement_jj_ps.pdf.

12. Nathan Leamer, "A Conservative Case to 'Raise the Age' in Michigan," R Street Institute, April 2016, www.rstreet.org/wp-content /uploads/2016/04/60.pdf.

18. Prisons as Nursing Homes: A Taxpayer Debacle

1. Florida Department of Corrections, "2017–18 Annual Report," http://www.dc.state.fl.us/pub/annual/1718/FDC_AR2017-18.pdf.

2. See Florida Statute Title XLVII 947.02, http://www.flsenate.gov /Laws/Statutes/2019/947.02

3 http://static-lobbytools.s3.amazonaws.com/press/73652_florida _taxwatch_florida_s_aging_prisoner_problem.pdf.

19. In Defense of Survival: Incentivizing Good Behavior

1. See Georgia Department of Corrections, *Orientation Handbook for Offenders*, www.dcor.state.ga.us/sites/all/files/pdf/GDC _Inmate_Handbook.pdf.

2. See Georgia Department of Corrections, "Standard Operating Procedures: Offender Discipline," November 6, 2017, www.powerdms .com/public/GADOC/documents/105928.

3. Georgia Department of Corrections, "Standard Operating Procedures."

4. Ed Chung, "Smart on Crime: An Alternative to the Tough vs. Soft Debate," Center for American Progress, May 12, 2017, www .americanprogress.org/issues/criminal-justice/news/2017/05/12/432238 /smart-crime-alternative-tough-vs-soft-debate.

20. Electoral Politics: The New Revolution

1. Christopher Uggen and Jeff Manza, "Voting and Subsequent Crime and Arrest: Evidence from a Community Sample," *Columbia Human Rights Law Review* 36 (2004): 193–215; Matthew R. Lee and Shaun A. Thomas, "Civic Community, Population Change, and Violent Crime in Rural Communities," *Journal of Research in Crime and Delinquency* 47, no. 1 (February 2010): 118–47.

2. Lewis Conway Jr., "Still Running!," *Medium*, July 27, 2018, medium .com/@lewisconwayjr/still-running-c9dd676e1196.

3. Opinion No. KP-0251, Office of the Attorney General of Texas, May 22, 2019, www.texasattorneygeneral.gov/sites/default/files/opinion -files/opinion/2019/kp0251.pdf.

4. "The Reconstruction Generation, 1870–1887," United States House of Representatives, History, Art, and Archives, history.house.gov /Exhibitions-and-Publications/BAIC/Historical-Essays/Introduction /Reconstruction-Generation.

5. Amy Kamp, "Austin First Fair Chance City in the South," *Austin Chronicle*, March 25, 2016, www.austinchronicle.com/daily/news/2016 -03-25/austin-first-fair-chance-city-in-the-south.

6. Madlin Meckleburg, "Lawmaker Seeks to Ban Local Laws That Remove Criminal History Question on Job Applications," *Dallas News*, December 13, 2016, www.dallasnews.com/news/texas-legislature /2016/12/13/lawmaker-seeks-ban-local-laws-remove-criminal-history -question-job-applications.

7. "Bill HB 577," Texas Legislature Online, capitol.texas.gov /BillLookup/History.aspx?LegSess=85R&Bill=HB577.

8. Anastasia Christman and Michelle Natividad Rodriguez, *Research Supports Fair Chance Policies* (New York: National Employment Law Program, 2016), www.nelp.org/publication/research-supports-fair-chance -policies.

21. Wards of the State

1. See also Arthur Longworth, "Raised, and Imprisoned, by the State," *Marshall Project*, May 26, 2015, https://www.themarshallproject.org/2015/05/26/raised-and-imprisoned-by-the-state,

2. Girls are disproportionately represented in the dually-involved youth population (foster and juvenile justice system-involvement). See Human Rights Project for Girls, Georgetown Law Center on Poverty and Inequality, and Ms. Foundation for Women, "The Sexual Abuse to Prison Pipeline: The Girls' Story," https://www.cclp.org/report-finds-troubling-link-between-sexual-abuse-and-prison, 24–31.

22. Mass Incarceration and Small Business

1. National Institute of Corrections, "Create a Culture of Offender Employment Readiness and Retention" in *Correctional Industries: A Guide to Reentry-Focused Performance Excellence*, 2019, info.nicic.gov/cirs/node/39.

2. Safer Foundation, "Safer Foundation Three Year Recidivism Study, 2008," saferfoundation.jellcreative.com/files/documents/Safer%20Recidivism%20Study%202008%20Summary.pdf.

3. Heather Long, "Where Are All the Startups? US Entrepreneurship Near 40-Year Low." money.cnn.com/2016/09/08/news/economy/us-startups-near-40-year-low/index.html.

4. Proverbs 29:18.

5. See Pelshaw Group, pelshaw.com.

6. John Milton, *Paradise Lost* (New York: Penguin Classics, 2003).

7. See Prison Entrepreneurship Program, www.pep.org; Defy Ventures, defyventures.org; Determination, Incorporated, sites.google.com/view/determinationincorporated/home; and 2nd Opportunity, LLC, 2ndopp.com/our-programs.

8. See Byron Johnson, William Wubbenhorst, and Curtis Schroeder, "Recidivism Reduction and Return on Investment: An Empirical Assessment of the Prison Entrepreneurship Program," *Baylor University*, www.pep.org/wp-content/uploads/2018/02/Baylor-2013-Study-of-PEP.pdf, 28. Author's calculations use the cumulative annual saving divided by the number of program participants studied to extrapolate per person cost.

9. See Georgetown University Pivot Program, pivot.georgetown.edu.

10. See Eric Westervelt, "From a Cell to a Home: Newly Released Inmates Matched with Welcoming Hosts," NPR, January 16, 2019.

23. A New North Star

1. See also Vera Institute of Justice, "Reimagining Prison in Germany and Norway," www.vera.org/spotlights/reimagining-prison-in-germany-and-norway.

2. Maya Schenwar, "America's Plantation Prisons," *Truthout*, August 28, 2008, www.globalresearch.ca/america-s-plantation-prisons/10008.

3. Mary Crowley, "How Connecticut Reimagines Prison for Young Men," Vera Institute of Justice, *Think Justice Blog*, March 24, 2017, www.vera.org/blog/dispatches-from-t-r-u-e/how-connecticut-reimagines-prison-for-young-men.

4. "The German Prison Program That Inspired Connecticut," *60 Minutes*, YouTube video, March 31, 2019, www.youtube.com/watch?v=yOmcP9sMwIE.

5. Maurice Chammah, "To Help Young Women in Prison, Try Dignity," *New York Times*, October 9, 2018.

6. National Employment Law Project, "Research Supports Fair-Chance Policies," August 2016, s27147.pcdn.co/wp-content/uploads/Fair-Chance-Ban-the-Box-Research.pdf.

About the Editors

The Reverend **Vivian Nixon** is executive director of College and Community Fellowship, a New York–based organization committed to removing barriers to higher education for women with criminal-record histories and their families.

Attorney **Daryl V. Atkinson** was the inaugural Second Chance Fellow for the U.S. Department of Justice, and is now the co-director of Forward Justice, a law, policy, and strategy center in Durham, North Carolina, dedicated to advancing racial, social, and economic justice in the United States.

Other titles of interest from The New Press

Not a Crime to Be Poor: The Criminalization of Poverty in America
Peter Edelman

Prison by Any Other Name: The Harmful Consequences of Popular Reforms
Maya Schenwar and Victoria Law

Prison Profiteers: Who Makes Money from Mass Incarceration
Edited by Tara Herivel and Paul Wright

Pushout: The Criminalization of Black Girls in Schools
Monique W. Morris

Race to Incarcerate
Marc Mauer

Rap on Trial: Race, Lyrics, and Guilt in America
Erik Nielson and Andrea Dennis

Start Here: A Road Map to Reducing Mass Incarceration
Greg Berman and Julian Adler

Understanding Mass Incarceration: A People's Guide to the Key Civil Rights Struggle of Our Time
James Kilgore

Until We Reckon: Violence, Mass Incarceration, and a Road to Repair
Danielle Sered

Usual Cruelty: The Complicity of Lawyers in the Criminal Injustice System
Alec Karakatsanis

Publishing in the Public Interest

Thank you for reading this book published by The New Press. The New Press is a nonprofit, public interest publisher. New Press books and authors play a crucial role in sparking conversations about the key political and social issues of our day.

We hope you enjoyed this book and that you will stay in touch with The New Press. Here are a few ways to stay up to date with our books, events, and the issues we cover:

- Sign up at www.thenewpress.com/subscribe to receive updates on New Press authors and issues and to be notified about local events
- Like us on Facebook: www.facebook.com/newpressbooks
- Follow us on Twitter: www.twitter.com/thenewpress

Please consider buying New Press books for yourself; for friends and family; or to donate to schools, libraries, community centers, prison libraries, and other organizations involved with the issues our authors write about.

The New Press is a 501(c)(3) nonprofit organization. You can also support our work with a tax-deductible gift by visiting www.thenewpress.com/donate.